Adult Teaching and Learning:
Developing your practice

Adult Teaching and Learning:

Developing your practice

Sue Cross

 **McGraw-Hill**
Higher Education

Open University Press
McGraw-Hill Education
McGraw-Hill House
Shoppenhangers Road
Maidenhead
Berkshire
England
SL6 2QL

email: enquiries@openup.co.uk
world wide web: www.openup.co.uk

and
Two Penn Plaza, New York, NY 10121-2289, USA

First published 2009

A catalogue record of this book is available from the British Library

ISBN-10: 0-33-523466-6 (pb) 0-33-523467-4 (hb)
ISBN-13: 978-0-33-523466-0 (pb) 978-0-33-523467-7 (hb)

Library of Congress Cataloging-in-Publication Data
CIP data has been applied for

Typeset by Graphicraft Limited, Hong Kong
Printed in the UK by Bell and Bain Ltd., Glasgow

Fictitous names of companies, products, people, characters and/or data that
may be used herein (in case studies or in examples) are not intended to
represent any real individual, company, product or event.

The McGraw·Hill Companies

This book is dedicated to all who have shared my commitment to adult learning and professional development at University College London: MA students, short course participants, colleagues, examiners and academic support staff. Thank you.

Contents

Acknowledgements   viii

1 **Introduction: Theory, practice and the elements
   of teaching**   1

2 **Real teaching and virtual learning: Learning
   environments, technologies and interactivity**   27

3 **Recognizing effective teachers: Professional
   identity, power and evaluation**   54

4 **Assessment: Functional analysis and a typology
   of individual difference**   81

5 **Positive approaches to participant wellbeing: Social,
   environmental and emotional factors in teaching**   111

6 **Learning outside the classroom: Informal and
   non-formal learning, motivation and flow**   133

7 **Conclusion: The professional character of the teacher**   160

References   165
Index   169

Acknowledgements

Grateful acknowledgements are due to Dr Elizabeth Shepherd and Dr Nicholas Grindle for commenting on early drafts of the text; also to Rev. Dr Christine Sorenson for commenting on a final draft. Professor Helen Weston, Dr Duna Sabri, Clare West and Rosalind Duhs gave expert comment on particular chapters for which I am most grateful. Any remaining errors in the text are, of course, my own.

Matthew Cross assisted in preparing the manuscript for publication. His professional competence and tireless enthusiasm for the whole project were crucial to its completion.

I am grateful to UCL for enabling me to spend some time writing at the Bundesinstitut für Erwachsenenbildung (St Wolfgang, Austria), where the staff and situation welcomed and inspired me. Finally, particular thanks are due to Dr Andrea Waxenegger, University of Graz, for encouraging me in this direction in the first place.

1 Introduction:
Theory, practice and the elements of teaching

Effective, enjoyable teaching is about knowing what to do (or refrain from doing) *and* being able to do it. It is about beginnings and endings, introductions and conclusions, process and content, absence and presence. It is about being authentically 'you' while also being totally engaged with other people: the learners.

Teaching, like other abilities, develops through a combination of thoughtful practice, reflection and stimulation. This guide is intended to provide some of that stimulation, introducing some key concepts and practical issues with a view to prompting critical reflection on your own practice – and perhaps pointing the way to new things to try. In particular, this book tries to explain *why* top teachers do things the way they do and *why* some aspects of teaching are not nearly as simple as they initially appear. It also underlines why a full conception of the idea of 'the teacher' is immensely valuable.

Getting a grip on learning and teaching in the adult context is arguably even more difficult than it is in the context of the child. In most cases, we at least have a common notion of what a teacher of children 'looks like' – but teaching adults means many different things to different people. Indeed, although this book is aimed at the 'teachers' of adults, I fully anticipate that readers may be drawn from any professional background. One of the fascinations of this field is that individuals from all walks of life find themselves required to engage in adult teaching and learning, bringing with them a huge variety of perspectives and experience. To meet this challenge effectively, they must nonetheless all become professional in their approach, whatever their job title – and, at heart, being professional begins with an appreciation of the values underlying the practice of teaching and an acquaintance with some of the big ideas. Whoever you are, therefore, this book has something for you.

Where to start? I could begin with a definition, or a summary of published research in the field, or a clever quotation. Yet teaching and learning are social activities – and teaching skill is often largely developed through legitimate peripheral participation in established 'communities of practice' (Lave and Wenger 1991), so it may be helpful to introduce the various areas in which I have worked, not least as a model of the very great expansion of opportunity and reorientation that exist for teachers.

Introduction to the author

I like teaching people to *do* things. Where there is a practical application to the subject of learning, the teacher gets the benefit of (more or less) immediate feedback as to whether the learning is happening. Even better, learner and teacher enjoy moments of success together, and share failures and frustrations. Both experiences are to be expected, as part of the inevitable 'messiness' of all learning. This process is both my passion and my profession.

I initially trained and worked as a comprehensive secondary school teacher, mostly teaching physical activities ranging from dance to dinghy sailing. The young people whom I taught never failed to stimulate, challenge, amuse and amaze me. Nevertheless, after about a decade in practice, the fundamental changes in British state education introduced in the 1980s led me to change career direction. A new political attention to education led to the introduction of the national (e.g. centrally controlled) curriculum, standard assessment tests and directed teacher time in state schools. So I looked for work in a further education (FE) college, teaching drama to young adults. In formal terms, I was entirely untrained for this new role (and certainly inexperienced), even though the students I taught were of a roughly similar age to those I had taught in school. I learned through experience or, in professional terms, as a self-directed (even 'autodidactic'), autonomous adult learner. Jargon aside, I gained a thorough experience of the value of adult learning in supporting, working round, and creating opportunities for, career change. From work in FE, I went to work for the local educational authority, mediating between educational policy and policy-makers, and professional teaching practice and teachers. Slowly, my focus moved to the professional development of teachers more generally.

As the agenda for change shifted from secondary to higher education, I moved to work at University College London (UCL), widening my field of work to include the provision of adult learning and professional development opportunities across the university. I also extended my engagement with the professional development of teachers, establishing UCL's Masters in Adult Learning and Professional Development, and then leading its Masters in Education. In this context, I have been privileged to work with a diverse group of people (including doctors, lawyers, clergy, members of the armed forces, social workers, museum curators, art historians, learning technologists, administrators, linguists, nurses, therapists, private sector trainers and developers, and instructional designers) but all engaged in the business of adult learning.

My professional life has thus revolved around learning, teaching and professional development; I have enjoyed opportunities to engage with these activities in all roles – as teacher, student and even 'organizer', 'policy-maker', 'procurer' or 'consumer' – and in the widest range of contexts, crossing disciplines, ages and geographical boundaries. These have included all four principal sectors of adult learning: higher education (HE), adult education, work-based learning, continuing professional development (CPD), and informal and community-based learning. This experience has given me ample opportunity to become expert in the practice of professional teaching.

I am also quite sure about how much I now enjoy teaching grown-ups, and especially working with learners who themselves are responsible for teaching or supporting the learning of others. Contributing to another person's learning is as rewarding a job as one can find anywhere.

Bringing practice and theory together

Theory is fundamental. A sound understanding of theory is essential to the development of a teaching professional. However, in many cases, theory – and the process of theorizing – may seem an ivory tower phenomenon, often apparently divorced from day-to-day practical experience. This book seeks to correct that impression. It provides a first interface between theory and practice, emphasizing the reflexive relationship between the two. (In other words, theorizing will influence practice and the act of bringing understandings from practice into dialogue with theory may, in due course, influence the theory itself.) It will help you to explore the assumptions which underpin current performance and encourage experimentation with new approaches. A consideration of theory without practice frequently leads to abstraction; practice without theory leads to the repetition of error and impeded development.

This book is not a textbook but a primer for further study, thought and professional reflection. In so doing, the book is consciously aligned with the thinking of Stephen Brookfield, who said:

> Theorizing should not be seen as a process restricted to the academy and the preserve of the intelligentsia, but rather as an inevitability of sentient existence. A theory is nothing more or less than a set of explanatory understandings that help us to make sense of some aspect of the world . . . Interpreting, predicting, explaining, and making meaning are acts we engage in whether or not we set out deliberately to do so, or whether or not we use these terms to describe what we do.
>
> (Brookfield, 2005: 3)

It must be underlined that there is a lot of theory out there. The study of adult teaching and learning can routinely draw on the fields of sociology, social psychology, psychology, social anthropology, education, philosophy, literature, history, theology, linguistics and so on. Each of these fields offers particular theoretical perspectives, at least some of which may be in competition with one another.

There is a serious question as to which bits of theory have been selected for inclusion in this book. Instinctively, one might assume them to be the 'basic' ones – but even the process of identifying core or basic theory is both challenging and contested. Many experts will come to different conclusions about which perspectives are essential. Use of theory is thus a selective task.

Considering the selection of theories, it is important to remember that the process is frequently (indeed, some would say inevitably) influenced by their compatibility with external factors (including policy goals to which the selector subscribes); outside the confines of pure academic study, theories are rarely judged or compared purely on their own merits. This observation is not a criticism: in attempting to select a good or important theory, one is almost always faced with the question 'is this a good theory *for*' some other purpose or '*by*' some other standard. Thus, in trying to identify the most 'important' theories, or the most 'helpful' theories – let alone the 'right' theory – we almost always end up having reference to something else.

A classic example of this phenomenon can be drawn from the very notion of theory and practice. To answer whether a particular theory is good, important or right, one frequently asks whether it is right *for* a particular form of practice. But individual opinion on the nature of teaching practice is in turn potentially influenced by other theoretical perspectives, as well as policy concerns, identity, personal history and so on. For example, even apparently simple questions in this context are hard to answer: is teaching a technical process or an art? There is a temptation for policy-makers, or those with *organizational* responsibility for the delivery of teaching or training (as opposed to those with *operational* responsibility, i.e. those at the sharp end), to see it in a purely *organizational* context: provided appropriate resources are supplied, and the system is properly managed, teachers will deliver a measurable and predictable learning 'product'. Equally problematic, there is a tendency (although perhaps not so uniform) among those concerned with the practice of teaching to see it as an art, incapable of quantification, and only imperfectly understood by the uninitiated. Neither of these caricatures is entirely true – but neither is entirely false. From personal experience, we can see that both descriptions have strengths and weaknesses, and that the rather stereotyped attitudes I have described are informed by a variety of factors, some rational and some irrational, some conscious and some unconscious.

For all these reasons, we might have some cause to distrust any person who presents a theory or meta-theory as an *answer*. As individuals, we will be inclined to find certain perspectives more or less convincing. We can all, however, find great value in theorizing as a *process* to assist us in understanding and improving our practice. Possession of a theory is not a God-substitute, providing a coherent and conclusive account for the entire 'universe' of teaching practice. For the purpose of facilitating effective practice, it may be better to conceptualize theory as an intelligent conversational partner, posing many questions and – only when we are very lucky – offering the occasional convincing answer.

Cullen et al. (2002) have produced one of the fullest overviews of pedagogic research in adult learning in the UK to date. It was written for the Economic and Social Research Council (ESRC) to help it to determine the future direction for the Teaching and Learning Research Programme, possibly the UK's largest investment in research into the education of adults. While its density means it is not an easy read, its excellence lies in three attributes: its coverage of the field; its attempt towards rendering manageable and comprehensible a highly complex, contested, dynamic academic field in a neutral fashion; and its presentation of adult learning as an under-researched field which is essentially practice driven rather than theory led:

> The key realities are: firstly, there is little established 'evidence base culture' in teaching and learning. Secondly, pedagogic understandings are shaped by different – and sometimes conflicting – patrimonies across each sector. Thirdly, however, there has been a significant – and complex – degree of 'interbreeding' between the sectors of post-compulsory education, and it is often difficult to attribute a particular set of pedagogic 'outcomes' to particular sources of evidence. Fourthly, practices are either grounded in the day to day minutiae of 'chalkface' learning delivery (and hence ungrounded in theory) or, conversely, are tied to a particular 'grand learning theory' and are unsubstantiated in practice.
>
> (Cullen et al. 2002: 3)

This book is not a critique of the study, nor a comprehensive overview of the field, nor the development of a meta-theory. Indeed, the study itself underlines that theory is not a panacea. In truth, effective teaching is dependent upon a wide variety of factors, some under the teacher's control and some not:

we cannot say anything concrete about 'what works' over and above the relatively banal . . . In summary, the evidence suggests that what works is dependent on factors like:

- whether the pedagogic approach and learning arrangements adopted are consistent with the socio-cultural context in which learning takes place;
- the motivation of the learners (although motivation, and in particular its relationship to 'learner-empowerment' remains a contested issue in the literature);
- the competencies of 'teachers' and 'mentors' in the new roles required by the 'new pedagogy';
- the extent to which the expectations raised by learning can be met outside the immediate learning environment (and particularly in relation to delivering on 'life chances' like job opportunities);
- the extent to which the teaching and learning process is geared towards the 'pace' of the learner;
- the extent to which learning arrangements address the particular socio-cultural characteristics and 'life world' of excluded groups;
- the goodness of fit between learning arrangements (and learning content) and the purposes of learning (for fun; to enhance self-esteem; to enhance the career).

(Cullen et al. 2002: 13–14)

In accord with the thoughts above, this book draws upon, and encourages consideration of, perspectives from a wide variety of contexts and disciplines. In the development of my own practice, key readings from within the field (Dewey, Maslow, Kolb, Knowles, Lave and Wenger, Rowland, Barnett, Cranton, Mezirow, and Brookfield) have ranged alongside those drawn from 'outside' disciplines such as theology (Ford), philosophy (Ryle, Ricoeur, Levinas), anthropology (Geertz), psychology (Goffman, Csikszentmihalyi, Jung, Furnham, Maslow), linguistics (Tannen) and critical theory (Bourdieu, Eagleton, Habermas), as well as ideas derived from the arts (visual and creative), popular culture and sport. Some of these influences will be reflected in this text; others may not. It is important to emphasize that adult learning and teaching is not just a matter of cognition, as the heavy emphasis in the literature on this aspect of theory seems to imply. Rather, the twin processes of learning and teaching are situated in a social, cultural, emotional and physical context. Failing to acknowledge this reality is problematic.

It is not necessary for readers of this book to study or master all of the sources which have been helpful to me. Although I will refer to them along the way, it will frequently be for the purpose of illustration rather than prescription. One might term the writers upon which I draw my theoretical 'family'. Very few individuals in this world have identical relatives (and, indeed, the diversity is rather refreshing) – but most of us are likely to suffer if we have absolutely no family at all. This guide will be successful if it poses the questions which help the reader to begin to search for their theoretical families.

Finally, it is worth remembering that family members do not necessarily have to agree with each other (although a certain amount of general sympathy may be helpful)! In confronting the rather dazzling array of potential theoretical perspectives, it is important not to let them become paralysing.

Dualisms in theory and practice – and how to handle them

At least in the intellectual tradition of western Europe, theoretical development can be helpfully analysed by exploring the idea of 'duality'. In the modern, binary world, there is even more of a temptation to declare that a thing is one or the other, on or off, 1 or 0. I do not think that is a universally helpful approach.

A common assumption is that theory develops 'dialectically': Thinker A proposes a theory and, either in response or independently, Thinker B suggests a competing theory. Sometimes, there is an inclination to say that one approach is 'right' and to reject the other: frequently, one might condemn this response as simplistic. In other cases, the clash of theories itself is thought to contain the seeds of a third theory, which might be seen as a 'compromise' answering the contradictions inherent to the first two. This core idea can be presented as a simple formula:

Theory A + Theory B → Theory A/B ('Theory C')

However, life is rarely this simple. Very often, Theory A and Theory B both have intellectual strengths and weaknesses, but are based on such fundamentally different approaches that a compromise is impossible. In such circumstances, any attempt to force a compromise does such violence to the underlying concepts that the compromise ceases to be meaningful.

Instead, it is often helpful to leave both Theory A and Theory B intact, and to work with them both. Rather than rejecting one out of hand, or sweeping difficulties under the carpet by creating an artificial 'third way', practice is more richly considered when examined stereoscopically, a process which uses two separate (and slightly different) perspectives to obtain a more three-dimensional view of the object of study.

In this context, we come to the idea of dualisms. The *Oxford English Dictionary* defines a dualism as 'a system of thought which recognizes two independent principles'. In philosophy, this has been a traditional approach to the question of existence, often reduced to the problem posed by the apparently fundamental distinction between mind and body. A dualistic approach contends that aspects of the mind may not be fully explained by sole reference to its physical properties while simultaneously acknowledging the common sense reality of the existence of the physical world. Any attempt to reconcile the two principles, or to say that one is 'right' and the other 'wrong', is largely illusory: instead, for practical purposes, the best solution is to acknowledge that both might be 'true' – even if the relationship between them is apparently inexplicable. The very same can be said of competing models of theory and practice.

A dualism is 'complementary but conflictual' (Porter 2003: 28). One does not have to interpret the idea of a dualism as destructive to the idea of 'truth'. Plato's approach to mind/body dualism envisaged two entities in constant strife; yet Aristotle could conceive a more cooperative function (Porter 2003), almost a symbiosis. The *taijitu*, a symbol of the notion of *yin* and *yang* central to certain Eastern philosophies (especially those of China, Japan and Korea), offers a useful visualization of the way apparent opposites are held in balance, joined (rather than divided) by the different directions in which they pull.

Recognizing the difficulty inherent in resolving the conflict between theories thus represents an opportunity – if we are minded to grasp it. We can choose whether to work in an 'either/or' way or a 'both/and' way. This book is firmly committed to the latter option. It demands that we assume responsibility for making qualitative, subjective judgements on the appropriateness of a particular approach to each new situation. As such, we must be committed to a genuinely reflective practice which weighs actual and potential benefits for teachers and learners against actual and potential costs for teachers and learners. A demanding task – and one which can engender feelings of great isolation – I believe it is the only professionally ethical and intellectually honest choice to make.

In the following pages, I present three common dualisms which pervade the teaching and learning of adults. In many cases, there is strong social or political pressure to consider them as alternate choices; in reality, I suggest that each half of these dualisms is vital to a proper conception of the teaching and learning process.

Teacher-centredness/learner-centredness

The importance of 'learner-centredness' is stressed in much modern discourse. Now applied at various levels, it is perceived as a positive value for national policy and classroom activity alike. It is frequently (if implicitly) contrasted with the idea of 'teacher-centredness', which is often cast in a negative light. Techniques identified as teacher-centred have come to mean all that is didactic, boring, self-serving and neglectful of the interests of learners, while those identified as learner-centred are presented as engaging, relevant and satisfying.

Genuine benefits have been gained from initiatives based on a perceived tension between the focus on teachers and learners (perhaps particularly in terms of quality assurance; see Chapter 3) but there have also been significant losses. Uncritical application of the idea has led to the deprofessionalization of teaching, which includes deskilling and loss of status, esteem, confidence and purpose. At its worst, it has contributed to a loss of identity coupled with a discordant feeling of generic culpability for many social problems. It is important to separate the political functions of the term from its use as a critique of teaching and learning practice.

On unpacking the idea of any teaching and learning experience which is centred solely on the teacher or the learner, difficulties immediately become apparent. A glance at an off-the-cuff list of teacher-centred and learner-centred experiences provides a good illustration.

'Teacher-centred' experiences	*'Learner-centred' experiences*
• A lecture or sermon	• Personally set learning objectives
• A speech	• Presentations made to peers
• An anecdote	• Peer feedback
• A joke	• Personal interest-based projects
• A demonstration	• Portfolio assessment
• A facilitated group activity	• Unfacilitated group activity
• A moderated debate	• Games
• A guided tour	• Journal writing

First, in terms of potential impact on learning, it can be said that these experiences are all neutral. Their positive or negative effect depends solely on their judicious selection in the circumstances, and the efficacy with which they are accomplished. A lecture can be gripping, inspiring and informative, or it can be tedious, depressing and impossible to penetrate. An unfacilitated group activity can be liberating, empowering and cause for reflection, or it can be bewildering, frustrating and vacuous. A lecture may be well suited for the transmission of esoteric, technical information but not necessarily for literary appreciation.

Second, identifying any given teaching and learning experience as teacher-centred or learner-centred is a more or less arbitrary judgement.

In reading the previous list, many of the classifications may seem open to dispute. It is easy to say in principle that a lecture is teacher-centred – but good lectures are rarely delivered for the lecturer's benefit. In the selection of subject matter, pitch and tone (quite apart from considering the possibilities for teacher–learner interaction), the lecturer is thinking of the learner's needs and interests. The true measure of a successful lecture is defined by the learner. The distinction between teacher-centred and learner-centred activities becomes even more contested when we consider the idea of facilitated group activities. These have plenty of opportunities for learner contribution, and for learner leadership – yet the teacher, facilitating the group, plays (among others) a gatekeeping and time-management function which, although relatively hands-off, may be highly influential. Can we really say that any effective teaching and learning experience is totally dominated by the presence of one party rather than the other? I would suggest that we cannot.

To preserve the meaning of a learner-centred or teacher-centred model, the only possible conclusion is that the terms relate not to the attributes of the specific activities employed but to the focus of the teacher's attention. A learner-centred teacher attends to the learner's needs and interests, rather than those of the teacher. At first glance, one could agree with this principle: surely, it is right that the teacher puts the learner first – teaching is an altruistic profession. Yet, on closer examination, some aspects of the idea of competing models become more problematic. Does any teacher put their needs first? Can you be a good teacher if you do so? If one concludes 'yes' and 'no' to these questions, then the idea that there are two models of teaching with different areas of focus becomes meaningless: instead, we have simply come up with indirect ways to describe 'good' (competent) and 'bad' (incompetent) teachers. We must assume, therefore, that the distinction is not meaningless, and therefore that the answer to the second question ('Can a good teacher put their needs first?') is 'Yes'. The only other course is to reason that the answer to the first question ('Does any teacher put their needs first?') is 'No', at which point the entire discussion becomes irrelevant.

We can reason that a 'good' teacher can, in some circumstances, put their needs first by recognizing their professional character. The teacher's entire professional focus is on communicating their field of knowledge with fidelity and accuracy to the learner in such a way that the learner is nurtured and supported, and is able to develop. If we were to describe an individual to whom the needs of the learner were completely abhorrent, such that they refused to make any consideration of them, that figure would quite simply not be a teacher at all. Equally, it is possible to conceive of circumstances when the teacher's focus upon the learner must be counterbalanced by other considerations relevant to their professionalism. The teacher must cater to and protect the needs of *all* their learners, for a start: what suits one learner may not suit another. Similarly, the teacher must protect the integrity of the subject matter too: some fields of study, on some occasions, require the learner to be challenged to work with the rigours of the subject, and not the other way around. The teacher must also have a care for their professional ethics: they must remain 'centred' in their own professional character, which includes attention to the learner's needs but with a degree of protective attachment.

This very brief analysis leads to the conclusion, therefore, that both teacher-centred and learner-centred models of teaching, if they have any meaning at all, are 'right'. To be learner-centred is to be a teacher. At the same time, learner-centredness is a necessary but not always sufficient condition for being a teacher. We should recognize that the two models are not in competition but represent a theoretical dualism. A good teacher holds the two concepts in creative tension, and their practice is shaped by the interplay of the two.

Given this conclusion, it might be asked why the rhetoric of learner-centredness has come to be such a big idea in teaching. The reasons are not hard to discern (the coincidence of a practical and a conceptual trend in politics and society) and illustrate the significant role that social, political and economic discourses can have in defining (or confusing) basic professional realities for teachers.

Conceptually, the idea of learner-centredness reflects the 'victory' of one theoretical perspective (postmodern understandings of epistemology) over its competitors: the challenge to the existence of the 'grand narrative' is also a challenge to the teacher in their traditional role as expert in disciplinary knowledge. Knowledge itself, perceived as decentred, situated and relativist, cannot be transmitted because the teacher 'knows' little or no more than the learner. The teacher, thus redundant, falls under suspicion as a mere wielder of power. We can in fact contest this perspective in two ways, however. First, it presupposes a total postmodernist victory. This is wrong on both an internal analysis, because its arguments against hegemony – the 'normalizing' dominance of a position which necessitates the subordination of another – forbid its validity as one in its own right, and an external one, because it is but one critical perspective, and by no means the last word. Second, it presupposes that the teacher must be redundant even within its own framework. This is wrong because, provided the postmodern teacher is transparent about their own role (or as transparent as humanly possible), they retain *a* valid opinion, if not *the* valid opinion in the classroom. Moreover, through the exercise of professional skill, and bound by relevant professional ethics, they can assist in unlocking the various opinions of the learners in the classroom, and facilitate the comparison and exploration of these differing perspectives in a safe and supportive space. Postmodernist critiques may challenge the hegemony of the teacher – but, in turn, the teacher is no less equal than others. The hegemony of the learner is equally contrary to the postmodernist spirit.

Practically, the notion of learner-centredness has been a convenient banner for a range of interests which arose from the development of the knowledge economy, and especially the technicization, marketization and commodification of education systems. In particular, distributed access across the population (or a town, university, school or classroom) to information networks – which is an expensive new form of infrastructure, entailing investment in physical plant, hardware and software – finds an easy justification in the idea that it 'frees' the learner from the shackles of the teacher. Although it is not intended to deny that this new infrastructure is an overall good, the reverse psychology that was necessary in order to sell it (teachers can sometimes impede learners) has had an effect.

The popularity of the notion of learner-centredness may thus be largely attributed to its value as a political tool for the achievement of certain objectives rather than as an individually sustainable conceptual model. On the other hand, the teacher-centredness/learner-centredness dualism is helpful as a reflection of the nature of the teaching and learning experience, which requires careful tailoring of all its constituent elements to the interests of all those involved. This theme underlies much of this book. We shall explore the various elements involved in the teaching and learning process in the second half of this chapter.

Models of deficit and abundance

We sometimes talk about teachers working to either a 'deficit' or an 'abundance' model. What exactly does that mean? How does it help us to plan and provide the best opportunities for learning?

You are likely to be most familiar with a deficit model. It is so common that it will generally pass unchallenged, appearing to be plain common sense. The idea is that people take part in classes in order to be taught something they do not already know. It sounds obvious, doesn't it? The reality, however, is that this is only one of many motivations for adults to engage with teachers. Sometimes called 'instruction', an example of working effectively within a deficit model from my own practice would be dinghy sailing. Students arrived in my class knowing nothing about how to rig and sail a boat. Over a number of sessions I taught them how to do it, and also why it worked that way (physics becomes more interesting for some learners when it helps them to understand what is happening to them and how to control it). I had been thoroughly trained to be able to do this efficiently, safely and in a way which was enjoyable for the participants. Used appropriately, deficit models of teaching can be very satisfying for learners and teachers.

A deficit model tends towards:

- An appreciation of knowledge as being constituted of information which can be transmitted
- Diagnostic measurement of aptitude for a programme of instruction
- Predetermined outcomes for the learning
- Recognition of individual achievement
- 'Constructive alignment' (Biggs and Tang 2007) of learners, teaching and assessment.

The apparent opposite is an abundance model, which is characterized by a concern with what the learners bring into the classroom themselves. Some deficit model theorists describe learners as 'empty vessels waiting to be filled'; abundance model theorists speak in metaphors of journey or growth (see Fox 1983); what comes out of the process is, more or less, the same as what went in, although it is changed and developed.

Abundance models of teaching are characterized by a different attitude to the learners, the teaching and the recognition of success. Confidence in the experience, autonomy and capacity for self-direction of learners may lead to a lesser emphasis on the transmission of predetermined content by the teacher. Instead, participants in the class may be expected to share their existing knowledge or ideas on a topic, and to research particular aspects of that topic for subsequent sharing with the group as a whole. The teacher's expertise may be located in her/his ability to manage a highly participative process. The learners may have a sense of being 'in control'; the more expert the teacher, the less they may appear to be doing. Excellent performance in this context is often about knowing when to refrain from action as much as how to take it. When they do come, interventions are generally light-touch and focus attention on the learners' own ability to find out what they want to know, rather than on virtuoso displays of the teacher's disciplinary knowledge or practical expertise. At its best, an abundance model of teaching does not draw attention to the teacher. Rather it highlights and celebrates the experience of everyone present in the room.

For all these reasons, although preparation for this kind of teaching is equally important, it is done differently (in practical terms, it is much more open-ended and speculative). The success of the new teaching will depend on the way it articulates with the participants' understanding of themselves and the models of professionalism, career and personal identity within which they already work. As a result, participants may not always notice expert performance by teachers operating in an abundance model: whereas participants will often be able to comment positively on the knowledge, presentation style, and so on of 'instructors', they may simply not notice how well a group has been facilitated.

An example from my own practice of this form of teaching would be a career and professional development course I run for mid-career scientists. Through a process in which they work with a tutor team and each other, they explore the options available to them, develop their ability to evaluate and choose paths to follow, learn ways to access information, discover their own preferences and so on. This particular model of teaching can be very demanding on both teachers and learners (the fineness of the distinctions involved requires a degree of concentration and experience in order to make the experience really work) but can ultimately be very powerful.

An abundance model will tend towards:

- An epistemology of socially situated and personally constructed knowledge
- Relatively open access to a programme of activities
- Learning outcomes which value autonomy and self-direction
- Inclusion of social learning
- Emphasis on facilitative (sometimes known as non-directive) methods
- Assessment which enables personal selection of ways to present material for examination, and is probably categorical (i.e. pass or refer (fail)) rather than being numerical (i.e. capable of discriminating finely between the performance of different participants in order to produce, for example, an order of relative merit).

Knowles (1980) has written, very influentially, on an abundance model of adult learning which he terms 'andragogy'. In fact, he draws extensively on an older, European tradition of *Volkshochschulen* (German for people's high schools, now generally used to mean adult education centres), which originated in the middle of the nineteenth century. This book does not accept the andragogic model without question, but its influence must be recognized and so references to it will occur from time to time throughout the text.

From this introduction, it should again be clear that neither an abundance nor a deficit model is the only 'right' answer. Both provide highly effective ways to conceptualize approaches to teaching and analysing the educational learning process but, again, they cannot be regarded as competing with one another. As a technical matter, it might be fair to say that these models are descriptions of regimes for practice rather than theories. A dualistic approach to them is helpful, however, not least as it underlines that teachers do not have to be confined to one or another. Although some subjects lend themselves strongly to one form (it is hard – and somewhat worrying! – to imagine an abundance model of driving instruction), they may often be used in concert in classroom contexts. An expert teacher may select one approach for one learning activity, and another for others; a combination of both, according to need, may be especially successful. The teacher should thus keep both models in mind in their practice.

Behaviourism and cognitivism

Behaviourism and cognitivism represent two grand theories, or 'super' theories, with great significance for adult learning and teaching. Between them, they provide a lens through which almost all teaching issues become clearer: they relate both to methods of teaching and perspectives on the nature of material being taught. In understanding the two, it also becomes much easier to recognize and deal with other relevant theoretical perspectives.

Behaviourism is one of the longest lived adult learning theories. Based on scientific experiments with animals (initially Pavlov's dogs, followed by Skinner's rats and Thorndike's pigeons), the theory drew upon observations of an enduring association between stimulus (such as a bell ringing when food is offered) and response (such as salivation at the sound of the bell even when no food is presented), a process which came to be known as 'conditioning' (bell rings; animal is ready to eat). Behaviourism concerned itself only with observable behaviour as evidence of learning, a scientific approach which was important in distinguishing psychology (the discipline within which behaviourism was born) from philosophy. This stance does limit the application of behaviourism to a certain extent, but its impact as a theory should not be underestimated. In particular, it offers an understanding of the teacher's agency (intentionally exercised or otherwise) in the learning process.

Behaviourism highlights the effects of systematic reinforcement on particular behaviours. Systematically rewarding the response you want from learners will increase the chance that they will continue to make that response. Behavioural approaches may be particularly relevant early in a new course while establishing the ground rules of behaviour during sessions. It is not unreasonable to suggest that a little basic 'training', even with adults, can be a welcome way of saving time, establishing group cohesion and reducing anxiety. We might consider, for example, establishing how references are to be cited in written work to conform to appropriate disciplinary conventions. This is not a negotiated practice (though its purposes, origins and effects can be open to debate), it is something which needs to be done. Similarly, conventions about time-keeping, use of mobile phones or laptops might be managed from a behavioural perspective. There are many ways in which conscious use of the technique may be appropriate, although there are also many contexts in which it may not be so. Much of the training in the armed forces, for example, is based on behavioural techniques: they are well suited to the process of ensuring that people will react in certain ways, or follow certain procedures unquestioningly, especially in high-risk circumstances. Behaviourism is not at all well suited, however, to teaching complex disciplinary knowledge or abstract concepts, such as an ethics course. In essence, behaviourism is well suited to procedural knowledge but it may be less well suited to anything but the most basic 'propositional' knowledge.

Teachers can also benefit from an understanding of behaviourism as a way of avoiding learner responses which are not desired. An awareness of behaviourist critiques brings with it an awareness of the consequences of one's own actions. Behaviourist theory applies not only to our intentional, conscious actions, but also to our unconscious ones: many examples of inappropriate behaviour are conditioned responses, either to something we have done or something done by someone else. We consider them 'inappropriate' largely because we fail to recognize the context to which they are related. For example, each time a student hands work in late and it gets marked without any loss of credit, the chance that work will be submitted late again is increased.

A number of researchers had their roots in behaviourist theory but developed work within the cognitive domain. Cognitive theories of learning are concerned with the mental processes which are associated with propositional knowledge ('knowing that . . .') and the development of what we perceive to be autonomous or self-directed learning by adults. Tusting and Barton (2006) provide a comprehensible introduction to the theories of learning which have their roots in the discipline of psychology. They say that cognitive theories of learning address the perceived weakness of behaviourism in that it does not really help us to understand how conceptual learning occurs, nor enable us to see how adults gain and enjoy autonomy in learning. They comment that:

> cognitivist approaches study the roles of individual, internal, information-processing elements of learning. The roots of cognitivist approaches to learning can be traced back to *Gestalt* psychology, which drew attention to the significance of questions

of perception, insight and meaning. In particular, it identified the importance of moments when learning reorganizes experience, so that the learner suddenly 'sees' the whole phenomenon under study in a new way.

(Tusting and Barton 2006: 6)

Cognitive accounts of learning are based around thought, and especially how thought and behaviour are linked. Until the development of sophisticated scanning technology, researchers could not learn much by watching people thinking; instead, cognitive theorists created models and taxonomies in order to explain and represent the mental processes associated with learning. Originally interested in the successful transmission of existing bodies of knowledge (both procedural and propositional), later variants of the cognitive model suggest that the learner is not a passive recipient of the content being organized and encoded for transmission. Models began to develop around the idea that learners actually construct new knowledge by working with that which they already have and adapting it to account for new information or by working with the new material to make it fit with what the learner already knows. These approaches belong within an important subset of cognitivist theory, known as constructivism (see Chapter 2).

Constructivism is an umbrella term for a clutch of theories which stress the importance of the active engagement of learners in their learning. In working with propositions, mediated through peers, teachers, technology, artefacts or environments, we adjust, amend and rebuild our knowledge and understanding of the world. As we do this we get better at doing it. We may even reach the point where a previously uninteresting and/or baffling field of knowledge becomes personally meaningful (see Chapter 6). Constructivists might tend toward abundance models of learning and teaching as people work together to enable the new learning to be developed through discourse on the chosen topic. Such discourse may generate multiple versions of the knowledge being constructed on a particular topic. Constructivists tend not to value rote learning or reproduction of teacher-generated material. They generally prefer to look for the ability of learners to evaluate critically their own, and each other's, statements. Evidence must be cited; bias or the privileging of a particular ideology need to be identified. Constructivist theory leaves room for the subjective and the personal response. As such, it is more commonly found within the humanities and arts disciplines than in the sciences, where positivism is still pretty much the dominant influence on learning and assessment. Constructivist methods are particularly suited to complex situations in which it is important for participants to work out for themselves appropriate courses of action.

They may not seem very efficient if you are tasked with training people to perform routine tasks in line with a set of procedures or protocols, nor would they be an ideal way to organize lifeboat drill on a ship.

Elements of teaching

The final section of this chapter (before looking at learning environments and the use of technology in Chapter 2) reviews the key elements of the teaching process. My analysis in this regard is not particularly distinctive: Rogers' (2007) introduction to adult learning provides a similar narrative, although in greater depth and length.

If you teach, you will certainly be familiar with at least some of the tasks which fit into each element. If you are in a 'learning support' role you will certainly be involved with at least some elements, if not others. For the sake of clarity in the text, however, I am going to assume that the 'teacher' does them all. In reality, in much of adult learning practice, the elements of teaching are distributed between several specialists who contribute to a teaching team. This can make schemes to reward excellent teachers more difficult to design and implement than some education policy-makers, or institutional managers would like them to be. We shall look briefly at this issue in Chapter 3.

The analysis of the teaching process I propose includes six elements. These are:

- Identification of potential learners, estimating their requirements, and breaking the ice
- Creation, selection and preparation of tasks, experiences and activities
- Preparation of resources
- Performance of tasks, roles and responsibilities
- Assessment and feedback on learning
- Evaluation and review of teaching.

Identification of potential learners, estimating their requirements and breaking the ice

The old saying that 'you can choose your friends but you can't choose your family' is also apt when thinking about the relationship between most learners and their teachers. Most teachers inherit learners allocated to them by another teacher or administrator. They are often stuck with each other and must negotiate an effective relationship to make the best of the situation. In the worst-case scenario, they may have to deal with 'baggage' acquired from other members of 'the family' and so be in a marginally less propitious situation to develop a positive working routine than mere strangers.

Experience of both postgraduate teaching and continuing professional development leads me to conclude that the most effective teaching acknowledges the integrity of the discipline being taught while recognizing the knowledge, understanding and experience appropriate to the adult status of the learners. So, assuming you have been selected to teach because you are (in at least some sense!) an expert on the topic of the learning, how do you prepare to engage with the people who will be your learners?

The important attributes of potential and new learners can be grouped in several ways, including the following:

- Physical/developmental characteristics such as age, gender, particular attributes relevant to the situation (e.g. size, weight and fitness if the learning involves physical activity)
- Previous experience such as fluency in the language of instruction, academic credentials and other qualifications, occupation
- Ability to pay the costs of the learning
- Need to benefit from the outcomes of the learning
- Understanding of what the learning will require
- Desire to know more or be able to do something better
- Membership of a group which more powerful people have decided needs to be trained.

Examining the factors listed above, it is clear that some imply a deficit or gap to be filled, and others imply an abundance of knowledge, experience and ability upon which to draw. Awareness of these factors can significantly help in planning teaching. Before a course begins, therefore, it is important to gather as much relevant information about participants as possible. This process may be achieved formally, competitively and expensively (for example, the administration of the GMAT (Graduate Management Admission Test) to likely entrants on prestigious MBAs) or it may be minimal ('Can you afford to pay the fee?'; 'Are you free on Tuesdays?'; 'What topic/module do you have to do next to satisfy the requirements of the programme specification?'). Whatever the context in which you work, successful teaching is often based upon good 'intelligence' about the learners. It will help you to design your opening activity ('You don't get a second chance to make a first impression') and help in creating an appropriate mix of activities to challenge and reassure or affirm the learners as the sessions progress.

When starting a new course, some learners may be apprehensive, and all concerned will certainly require the opportunity to acclimatize to the new situation. In such circumstances, it is worth using short, intro-ductory activities (ice-breakers) to facilitate this. (For related reasons, although with the goal of consolidating the learning experience rather than creating its foundations, teachers should also give some thought to closing activities.) It is essential that all learners feel that you want them to be there. There is merit in demonstrating this in practical ways, perhaps by contacting or meeting them beforehand (by email or by send-ing copies of relevant handbooks with joining instructions), or by phone, or face-to-face interview. If the latter, structure it so that the new learner realizes you are interested in putting them at their ease, rather than simply wanting to judge them.

Although strategies for initiating teaching vary considerably and different teachers will tend to adopt (with equal validity) different approaches, it is worth highlighting one issue which, if it crops up, will often affect the attitude of new learners regardless of the skill of the teacher's initial actions. 'Conscripted' participants, or those who (for what-ever reason) are not beginning the course entirely voluntarily, are likely to behave differently from voluntary participants, even if they have the best of intentions. The exercise of power frequently engenders a feeling of resistance, even in individuals who would otherwise be positively dis-posed to the learning, and this can manifest itself in unexpected ways. The most overt manifestation can be behaviour directly challenging the integrity of the group or the authority of the teacher; more subtly, pas-sive resistance or truculence can quietly poison the atmosphere of a group and inhibit the formation of good relationships. This behaviour will require the intervention of the teacher: learner disengagement of this type is unlikely to go away on its own. You should think carefully about how, and when, to explore any grievance the relevant learner(s) may feel they have. Manifesting a degree of empathy, listening to and understanding the learner's problem, and assisting them in exercising their own agency within the context of the classroom may go a long way to restoring their commitment. At the very least, it reaffirms your role as 'teacher' and forms the basis for future discussions in resolving the conflict in which they find themselves.

This may seem a rather gloomy note upon which to start – but it high-lights an important point. Knowles (1984) articulated a conception of the adult learner as self-directed, internally motivated, interested in prob-lem solving, and the guardian of a stock of prior learning which can be a resource for current study. It is unclear, however, if he meant that all adult learners exhibit these characteristics (i.e. these qualities define what it means to be an *adult*, rather than a *child*, learner) or that teachers of adults should seek to provide opportunities for adults to become like this at some point in their lives. Experience of my own learning as an adult, and experience as a teacher of many others, leads me to believe that, while Knowles was right to articulate these attributes as one model of adult *potential* (there are others too: Gilligan (1982) proposes that women's development into maturity might be characterized very differently), it is certainly not the case that all adults exhibit them all or even some of the time. Even the most confident self-directed and autonomous learner may have their ability to work within their normal spectrum of responses disrupted by the unplanned aspects of a situation (see Chapters 4 and 5). Others – including the 'conscripts' to learning – may require a great deal of support before they can even identify with his concept, much less manifest it. Teachers may also find that a room containing several learners who are particularly strongly self-directing is hard to manage for the benefit of all the other participants too.

Creation, selection and preparation of tasks, experiences and activities

Teaching should be *eventful*. Good teaching can be characterized by the fact that it includes remarkable, astonishing, amusing or affecting things. To a certain extent, teaching is showmanship with a serious purpose. The content of teaching matters but, if learners are not paying attention, it is likely to have no impact. Some teachers, particularly inexperienced ones, spend too much of their preparation on rehearsing their own understanding of the content and not enough time preparing for the *event*. Content matters – but delivery does too.

Active engagement with the content is also important. Despite what we may like to assume as teachers, the greatest influence on learning success is the amount of time learners devote to purposeful engagement with the material to be learned, and the timely and accurate feedback they receive on their performance (Coffield et al. 2004). In other words, no matter how eloquent the delivery, or well argued the point, one of the biggest factors contributing to success is 'time on task'. As a result, teachers should be alive to the myriad options for stimulating (or requiring) learners to engage actively with the relevant content through the use of appropriately designed activities.

In considering strategies for presentation, as well as potential activities, teachers may benefit from overtly considering the sensory experience that the learners will have of the session. Despite the primary school overtones, successful teaching is vivid teaching: if there is a relevant way to maximize the sensory input, it is worth considering. Providing a varied diet of activities is similarly beneficial. When working at a distance from learners, teachers may need to pay particular attention to the way in which activities are structured, and the form in which instructions are given, so as to make them meaningful in a more detached context. It may also be beneficial for the teacher to ask themselves whether the activities set can assist the teacher in the exercise of their role. Might they comprise an opportunity for formal or informal assessment, and the giving of feedback? Might they comprise an opportunity to learn about the learners, either to get to know them better or to monitor their state of wellbeing? Might they serve as a stimulus to reflect upon the teacher's own professional competence?

Preparation of resources

Beyond emphasizing the importance of being well prepared for teaching, there seems little to say about preparing resources. Yet a full conception of the face-to-face teaching experience draws upon a range of resources not normally considered: thinking about what you may need represents another opportunity to think about what you want to do, and what circumstances may intervene.

In preparing for a teaching session, it is thus worth asking at least the following questions. You may come up with more. For those working in the institutional context, an awareness of the answers to these questions may also be of value should auditors inquire.

1. What resources will the teacher require?
2. What resources will the participants require?
3. What purpose do the resources serve?
4. What will they enable the teacher and learner(s) to do in relation to the material or content? (That is, will they enable new material to be introduced? Recorded and reinforced? Will they enable existing knowledge to be remembered and rehearsed?)
5. What resources might assist the teacher in gaining and sustaining attention, stressing importance, rewarding, diverting (not distracting), amusing or entertaining the learner(s)?
6. How will ephemeral resources of time, atmosphere, goodwill be used?
7. What will the teaching environment be like? Is there a deficit to overcome (no windows!) or will it be abundant with possibilities?
8. If the space is abundant (e.g. some high-tech teaching rooms with loads of gear) does it raise the wrong expectations in the learner(s)? Or the teacher? Beware the temptation to use toys and facilities solely because they are there.
9. Are resources available to cover the unexpected? How does the teacher serve the needs of learners who arrive late, leave early

or do not come at all? Must resources be provided to cover what
has been missed?

10. What will the resources cost? Who pays?
11. What resources may the learners be expected to bring, and
how may they be used? (My favourite recent contribution
from a learner is a little yellow rubber duck which squeaks when
squeezed. Combined with a box of sweets, the duck was used
to give an excellent introduction to behaviourism and its
impact on learning.)

This list of questions is by no means exhaustive; before completing their
preparations, teachers should know the answers to most of these, and
perhaps to others. Reflection upon those answers gives clues to personal
theories of teaching: as a rough rule, what someone takes the trouble to
prepare and provide they value. Certainly, the provision of resources does
send (consciously or otherwise) a tangible message to learners about personal priorities: my favourite educational theory session for MA students
began with games and a picnic! My rationale was that the learners need
to understand that theory is not necessarily boring, hard, or both.
Sometimes a playful approach to serious issues can be rewarding.

Performance of tasks, events, roles and responsibilities

Teaching is a performance art. Teachers do many things whose only
purpose is to enable other people to learn, whether those people are
physically present or otherwise. Teaching is very different from merely
covering the syllabus or transmitting information. One illustration
comes from my own past, while I was attending a course for the purpose of professional development. I was allocated to Quentin's class a
long time ago, but I remember this particular session very clearly:

Quentin's class regularly began, after the coffee break, in the
middle of a session which ran from 6 p.m. to 9.30 on Tuesday nights
for three terms. Most of the students, including myself, were
school teachers voluntarily taking additional academic qualifications. Quentin's lectures always began on time and proceeded in
a carefully structured and thoroughly prepared way to cover the
topic scheduled for the lecture.

On one occasion, an unfortunate coincidence of circumstances
(the over-running of other lectures and insufficient cafeteria facilities to process 100 thirsty learners expeditiously) caused all of
Quentin's class to be late arriving for his lecture. We arrived, only

> to discover Quentin in full swing, delivering the lecture to an empty room. We thought (as fellow teachers) that he was making an ironic point; surely, as the room filled quickly, he would stop and begin the lecture again, even if we were admonished for our time-keeping. But, no! Despite the fact that the late arrival was plainly not a result of individual error, and that this was a core course, he carried straight on to the end of his lecture and completed the session precisely on schedule. He duly left. There had been no inter-action between Quentin and us, his learners, at all.

Working within an extreme interpretation of a deficit model of teaching, Quentin demonstrated an extraordinary lack of concern for the circumstances in which the learners were trying to learn. There may have been many reasons why Quentin resorted to the behaviour he adopted – but he did not explain them to us. From that point on, many of the students gave up on his class; of those who did continue to attend, many were pretty well disengaged. Teachers are of great value because they are more than mere resources to be accessed by learners: their dynamism is caught up in the professional persona they choose to adopt, and the way in which they present themselves and their subject.

There is no shortage of literature on how to tackle the basic activities likely to be required of teachers (see, e.g. Rogers, A., 2007, Rogers, J., 2001). Nonetheless, it is important – and largely the object of this book – to question why any particular teaching practice (whether recommended by a book, senior colleague, learner, etc.) is useful or beneficial and whether this holds true in the particular circumstances it will be used. This process of reflexivity, which may be understood as the critical awareness of the assumptions that underlie practice (Tennant 2006), is absolutely crucial in turning performance from a mere show to the purposeful, professional activity of the teacher.

Assessment and feedback on learning

Many contributors to the teaching team may undertake the first four elements of the teaching process. It might be argued, however, that the most important professional responsibility for teachers is to be able to make proper judgements on the quality of learners' work.

Assessment can seem both technical and rather obscure but acquaintance with the basic principles illustrates that it is both a vital component of teaching and learning, and even rather intriguing. Assessment is the crucial precondition for feedback, which helps learners to know what is going on in the learning process. It motivates them to sustain the learning when it is hard or unrewarding, tells them how far they have progressed (which they may not always be able to recognize for themselves), and helps them know where to go next. Research indicates that timely and accurate feedback on performance ranks as one of the most important factors likely to influence the effectiveness of learning. On first acquaintance, it might be thought that it would be a very straightforward thing to provide this kind of information to learners. It becomes complicated, however, when the purposes of assessment become unclear.

The process of assessment and feedback can, however, encourage dependence on the teacher (inhibiting the development of those often celebrated adult characteristics of autonomy and self-direction); it can mislead and discourage, and it may be used to exclude people from access to resources and activities. Chapter 4 will not only include more detail on how to use assessment to support individual learning, but also contextualize the process within the professional role of the teacher. We are frequently asked to serve several masters when we assess student learning and this can lead to considerable role conflict for teachers.

Evaluation and review of teaching

It is important to stand back from the work that we have done, and consider it in perspective. Here is where our abilities to engage as reflective practitioners come to the fore. We may do this after every session and/or at the end of a group of sessions or a 'module' or programme. We may be required to do it in certain ways for external audiences and we must do it for ourselves to feed the knowledge into the planning of more teaching. We might use a model like Kolb's (1984) experiential learning cycle.

Donald Schön's (1991) work on reflective practice has had a considerable influence on the way we consider the work of teachers who are responsible for the professional development of medical, educational and architectural practitioners for example. He, among others, identified a crisis of confidence in the way professionals in western societies were undertaking their responsibilities. In addressing this deterioration of confidence in professional expertise, he argued that effective practice goes beyond technical competence. Society expects professionals to ground their practice in an appropriate evidence base, and also to display the kind of 'professional artistry' which incorporates subtle adjustments in the light of the ongoing experience of the work in hand.

The need for evaluation, for evidence, can have practical implications for teachers. Earlier, we briefly referred to the importance of good closing sessions for teaching, as well as good openings. Good closings provide an opportunity to be explicit about what has been achieved during the session or activity. They can be carefully designed and precise, or have the energy and immediacy of a 'hot debrief'. They will motivate learners to continue with relevant activities and encourage them to feel positive about the prospect of returning for the next session or a new module, as well as also providing the teacher with immediate feedback on how the session went. Some teachers routinely ask for brief written feedback at the end of every session (a short structured questionnaire can be good for large groups to hand in as they leave). I often use self-adhesive notes for groups of medium size at the end of a two-day intensive course of professional development, inviting them to leave an anonymous note under the title 'Dear Tutor . . .'. The limit on space and time means we tend to get one or two ideas from each person; over the years, this has become useful feedback to the course team. It helps us to review how well the course has gone and to match participants' perceptions of it alongside our own. By using the same approach on many occasions we can also spot some trends emerging and plan amendments to the programme as required.

2 Real teaching and virtual learning:
Learning environments, technologies and interactivity

Good teachers have always used appropriate technology. They aim to ensure that learning is enhanced by any available means: shadows on a cave wall, loaves and fishes, paintings on rock, slates and chalk, papers and crayons, the written word, or the stars in the night sky. These are all examples of 'learning technologies', which we might define in general as objects, found or constructed, which may be used to sustain, enhance or change the experience of learning. Technological innovation has always changed society; it has never simply served it. So it is the case that the advent of modern communication and information technology (C&IT), and its extraordinarily rapid pace of change and development, has not only facilitated new ways of communicating information between learners and teachers but also contributed to new understandings of the way we think, express our thoughts and work together to learn. A brief exploration of constructivist theory (see below) is useful in order to appreciate this development: computing has interacted with constructivism as constructivists have recognized the potential to use computers in learning. Such an approach to learning has impacted on teaching methods and practices.

Working in partnership, learning technologists and teachers may find considerable synergy. Learning technologists work to provide a range of technological choices for teachers and learners. They vary in their specific approach (most commonly, they are either interested in solving a recognized problem by technological means; motivated by the intrinsic interest of the technology to develop solutions to problems which may not have been found yet; or interested in the transplanting of a technology from one field into another) but are generally united in not devoting a great deal of thought to the evaluation of the relative advantages and disadvantages of the various choices they generate.

The different emphasis offered by their professional backgrounds fosters a dynamic, creative and appropriately critical approach to their work. However, where an imbalance arises in their respective influence and freedom of action, problems can emerge.

More broadly, it must be acknowledged that there is a danger of loss of perspective in the way the learning technology is actually used. This chapter argues that excellent teaching can incorporate a whole variety of material and electronic resources for learning, as circumstances require – but it is the appropriateness of the technology to the particular teaching process which should be the governing factor in its selection. The novelty of a technology or tool does not necessarily make it appropriate. In this context, teachers must consider who purports to make the necessary evaluation about the relevance of particular technologies for learning; the professional character of the teacher (which comprises a commitment to ethical standards, a thoughtful and reflective approach to practice, and so on) should mean that they are the best qualified to exercise the ultimate discretion, albeit with the benefit of expert advice from learning technologists. Economies of scale may mean that the decision to 'buy into' a particular system must be resolved at an institutional, rather than a classroom level – but the teacher must retain the capacity to judge whether use of the new facility that has been made available is within the best interests of the learner(s) and the learning. (Reminiscent of the discussion in Chapter 1 with regard to the idea of learner-centredness, the teacher's judgement should not be swayed simply by the fact that the employment of a technology will give the learner an additional option which *may* assist some of them; the teacher must consider whether the existence of that option, and the possibility of it being exercised or not, will enhance or detract from the learning process as a whole. Potential impact on teacher workload is one obvious example: particular technologies, such as the use of virtual discussion boards can sometimes imply an open-ended commitment for teachers to respond on demand to an enormous population of learners without triggering a corresponding reduction in other professional obligations. As a result, the teacher is at risk of failing in one or more aspects of their professional duty, to the potential detriment of learners. Learner expectations need to be managed, or the interaction may become overwhelming or disappointing.)

Related to this notion, one of the revolutionary qualities of modern C&IT is the extent of its reach. Questions relating to the use or non-use of computer-based learning technologies are not simply the preference of one tool over another; C&IT's networking ability means that its use not only alters some of the ways in which the learning process is mediated but also shifts the essence of most interaction to a whole new environment. Selection of the choice of learning environment has traditionally been the more or less sole (if little regarded) prerogative of the teacher; by definition, where they choose to physically locate themselves with their learners, there the learning environment must be. Networked technology, however, offers the possibility for teachers to be drawn into situations where they are responsible for learning that takes place in an environment not of their choosing, and not entirely within their control. This can severely limit their opportunity to exercise professional discretion, and therefore their competence. Training in the use of new technologies, if provided at all, is often limited to the practicalities of accessing basic functionality and rarely includes pedagogic critique of the potential gains and losses associated with the change to teaching and learning practices.

At best, learning technologists and teachers can work constructively together in just about all situations where adults learn. Their aims occasionally coincide exactly; more often, they at least overlap. As a result, some practitioners who were led to adopt the professional character of both may now be hard pressed to know which category best fits them; for others, the professional character of each will remain distinctive. Both groups of people may, however, benefit from reading this chapter, which is relevant to the practical business of working effectively with the best technical support for learning. We should resist the vision advanced by some that teachers have simply become learning technologists, or that learning technologists are, *ipso facto*, teachers. While there is much that the two have in common, their aims, values and priorities remain essentially different.

At the risk of drawing generalizations which may be subject to criticism, learning technologists tend to be experts in the technical development and use of innovative (primarily computer-based) technologies for learning. Although they may have an appreciation of the practice of teaching and learning, it is generally not their main area of expertise, nor is it necessarily supported by a substantial amount of 'coalface' experience as teachers. The professional identity of the learning technologist is thus distinct from that of the teacher. This fact is more or less acknowledged by the Association for Learning Technology (ALT), an organization formed in 1993 which introduces itself on its website as 'the leading UK body bringing together practitioners, researchers, and policy makers in learning technology'. It expressly acknowledges its aspiration to support 'the professionalization of learning technologists'. Such a statement clearly reflects a shared view among its members that they have a unique professional identity which needs to be articulated, enhanced and communicated to colleagues in other fields.

Both e-learning enthusiasts and teachers who prefer to work in the physical presence of their learners generally appreciate the benefits of an approach known as 'blended learning'. The term describes the appropriate combination of the benefits which both material and virtual environments have to offer. In practice, however, this is not necessarily simple to achieve – especially if the learning process is to remain cost-effective. The policy pressure to replace some parts of real-world teaching with e-learning tools contributes to this difficulty. My own experience indicates that use of C&IT can indeed substantially enhance my teaching, but with the consequence of using more resources (time and money), rather than less. To a certain extent, these costs are presently hidden (absorbed by teachers working out-of-hours to generate appropriate material, answer emails and so on) but this model is not sustainable, and may be downright misleading to those who seek to evaluate the utility of learning technologies. Where institutions are unable or unwilling to meet these costs, teachers must exercise their professional judgement to ensure that learners get access to the best teaching and learning experience permissible within the scope of the resources available. 'Designing the teacher out' of learning systems does not represent the best value solution. It is true that some large-scale, content-rich, stable learning may be delivered effectively by a teacher-free e-learning programme, but many attempts to do so either have not been evaluated or have failed to meet their objectives. The notable exception to this is probably the use of e-learning to train people in the use of computers. It is not wise to generalize from that particular, however: the fact that people already motivated to study the use of computers benefit from using computers to access learning is hardly surprising (it is also true that those who wish to learn to sail benefit from spending considerable time in a sailing boat, but I do not expect all other learners to want to do so). Their success can be explained as much by their greater practical engagement with the subject of the study, as much as by the method by which they were taught.

Constructivist models of learning and their implications for teaching

Constructivist understandings of learning have had a significant impact on contemporary practices in the teaching of adults (even though most of the original work of pioneers in this perspective was undertaken while working with children). As briefly introduced in Chapter 1, constructivism can provide an insight into learning which accords with recent, socially informed approaches to understanding knowledge and its creation. Formerly, in relatively stable societies, the essence of education was seen as the transmission of existing knowledge to the next generation: it was desirable to ensure that this occurred without degradation or corruption of important texts. This learning objective was matched by the development of appropriate learning technology: the Gutenberg printing press, introduced around 1450, meant that scholars reading the Christian Bible in different parts of the Holy Roman Empire could have an increased degree of confidence that they were all reading the same text. Previously, copies were written by hand and individual errors might never come to light due to the difficulty of effectively comparing several copies.

The modern period in western society has been characterized by rapid and extensive change, however. Learning is now perhaps less concerned with ensuring that traditional wisdom is passed on; instead, emphasis is placed on the way learning enables people to adapt what they know to rapidly changing circumstances. Constructivist theories concern themselves with knowledge creation within individual minds and through social activity.

Piaget, Bruner and Vygotsky are acknowledged as the founding fathers of this way of understanding learning. Piaget is often described as a cognitive developmentalist because he observed the way children of different ages appeared to demonstrate a fixed sequence of stages in the development of their thinking. We can also think of him as an early constructivist because he realized (like Bruner) that the children were not just absorbing chunks of information, more or less passively (like sponges); rather, they were actively engaged in the process of their own learning. It was an important step for Piaget and later constructivists to see the learner as actively reconstructing knowledge in their own minds. Constructivist theorists propose that in doing this, the mind itself is also changed. Piaget's key concepts of 'accommodation' and 'assimilation' describe aspects of this process of cognitive adaptation.

Developmental approaches which were initially interpreted in a rather rigid and deterministic way have come to be seen as more indicative and pliable. People do not all seem to progress through all stages in the same way. Linearity has given way to recursivity. In other words, learners sometimes seem to go backwards and forwards (or, indeed, round and round) during the process of learning. Some people do appear inclined or able to learn incrementally (i.e. step by step) yet others do not: they may appear to be making no progress, and then move forward in a large and apparently unpredictable way. Incrementalism tends to be more comfortable for teachers as it provides them with reassurance about the efficacy of their own practice: they can see how the learner is progressing. Non-incremental learning, however, can look very much like failure, at least in the short term – and there is potential for misjudged interventions by the teacher (particularly by dismissing the possibility that the learner will, in fact, turn from 'ugly duckling' to swan) to bring about the very failure they prophesy. For obvious reasons, it can be very hard for teachers to identify where and when non-incremental learning may be going on; the key indicator, however, is the learner themselves. Especially in the adult context, the learner may be able to draw upon their previous educational experience to give an insight into the way they tend to behave. If all other factors are equal (see Chapter 5), a high degree of educational aspiration coupled with relatively low or other-wise flawed attainment may be an indicator. Rather than seeking the reassurance of straight-line development, teachers of non-incremental learners should instead look out for evidence of 'escape velocity': a rising curve of educational attainment as the pieces fall into place. They should focus their efforts on supporting the learner's self-confidence and making sure that evidence of attainment of necessary learning out-comes does not occur too late in the learning process for the individual to realize their ambitions.

It may be no accident that Piaget (working in a western, capitalist society) developed cognitive constructivist approaches focused largely on individual development while Vygotsky (working in the Soviet Union) placed much less emphasis on developmental stages in individuals, focusing attention on the social aspects of learning. Most importantly, he suggested that a child (and, by implication, later an adult) learns when, through interaction with a 'more knowledgeable other', progress is made with a task which is beyond the current ability of the learner. The construction of new knowledge occurs in this way at the Zone of Proximal Development. Through social interaction, the learner is able to tackle a task which is beyond her/his current capacity. This emphasis on the importance of other people (to observe in action, to engage in discus-sion or for emotional support) is central to the group of perspectives which nest under the heading of social constructivism.

The idea of 'scaffolding', which many teachers employ to concep-tualize their practice, originated in this theoretical territory. It describes the way in which people, including the teacher, act and speak to sup-port the learning activity in progress: learning is seen as a transition which often needs support while it takes place. Once the new knowledge has been integrated into the existing framework, the learner will be able to work independently with it, and the supportive framework can be removed. This framework may be precisely designed into a sophisticated learning programme (see below) or it may be imperceptibly embedded within cultural practices refined through long use by members of dis-tinct communities.

Learning can occur, of course, when people interact not in a formal learning environment but in vocational, domestic and social contexts. Indeed, concern with learning in those other contexts may be a develop-ing modern theme (see Chapter 6). Lave and Wenger (1991) describe the way diverse groups in varied societies induct new members. These informal 'apprenticeships' suggest that learning is more effective and sophisticated when it takes places in the actual context to which it applies. This idea of 'situated learning' uses the shared culture of 'teacher' (who is an expert practitioner in the discipline) and learner (the apprentice) to fulfil the scaffolding function. This shared culture is called a community of practice. Learning may be mediated by processes Wenger (1998) describes as 'participation and reification': the way people interact daily with each other and, by the use of artefacts, systems and processes to facilitate and record the conventions of their common practice. In accounting for the apparent success of new learning technologies in teaching applications related to C&IT, it is worth questioning whether this is a result of the online teaching structure or an example of situated learning in action.

In general, constructivists are interested in ways in which teaching uses material and symbolic 'objects' (including people in general, and the learners themselves) to enable learners to engage actively with acquiring, adapting and interpreting information in order to render a changing and uncertain world meaningful. This way of thinking is potentially important for both face-to-face teaching methods and e-learning, which may be asynchronous or conducted at a physical distance or both. Opportunities for interaction with simulated situations, the manipulation of material and/or virtual objects and individualized pathways through textual material permit learners to search and combine sources to suit their own requirements. Such activities provide examples of tasks designed to enable constructivist learning.

The increased opportunities that new learning technologies may offer for interaction and access to material may make them appear well suited to support for a constructivist model of learning. Mere creation or supply of the 'learning objects' (either material or virtual) does not, however, guarantee that learning will take place. A fuller reading of the relevant theory emphasizes the extent to which expert guidance remains vital to facilitation of the learning process; in the context of the examples we have considered, either by sustaining the 'centre' of the community of practice, or by assisting learners in navigating through the unpredictable, unmapped developments of the learning process. Teachers continue to exercise an important influence. They design tasks and activities, integrate appropriate assessment, provide relevant feedback (in person or integrated into the activity or task itself) and act as facilitators of dialogue and/or online moderators during the learning process. In general, they manage the learning environment to optimize it (as far as practicable) for the needs of the particular learners with which they work. Their ability to do so effectively is a significant indicator of the appropriateness of the environment to the teaching process.

The influence of learning environments

The 'physical' qualities of the environment, real or virtual, in which teaching takes place may make a substantial impact on learning. At best, individual teachers are in a position to establish the basic requirements, and then tailor the environment precisely to meet the needs of learning and learners. At worst, there is an expectation that all participants should put up with inappropriate facilities and make do with whatever happens to be provided. Wide variations in quality of provision may be caused by sectoral, institutional, departmental or disciplinary differences, as well as (to a certain extent) by good or bad fortune. While it is the case that effective teachers can overcome a substantial proportion of environmental disadvantages, it is important to highlight the benefits which arise from working in an appropriate environment. The most significant benefits are the scope for enhanced instructional design, and the physical comfort and boost in confidence which comes when learners feel their needs are important to the providers of the learning opportunity. Appropriate learning environments also reduce wear and tear on teachers, putting to better use considerable time and energy which would otherwise be spent in trying to overcome the shortcomings of the environment. If the group meets in a different place for each session, or if resources have to be transported around various buildings, the effect on the teacher is surprisingly significant. It is much easier to teach well in an appropriate space, which becomes home for the learners and is well appointed in terms of the facilities and resources it needs.

Conceptions of the resources required in a learning environment are often overly technicist. It is, of course, obvious that certain fields of learning require particular facilities. Formal educational institutions may be very effective in providing laboratory or technical equipment (which may be eligible for special funding), as required. The unavoidable nature of the investment is well understood. Discursive fields (such as the arts and humanities), on the other hand, generally receive little resourcing priority: their requirements appear so basic that many of those not involved in the education process (although at least partially responsible for its outcome: estate managers and timetablers, for example) assume that almost any space will do. In my experience, this is far from true.

The learning environment's important influence on teaching and learning has traditionally received little attention in educational literature, although recent years seem to have marked a growing interest. In reviewing the available material, it is important to distinguish between research, practitioner literature and sales or promotional material. A practical example will illustrate what I mean by this distinction. You may find an article in a scholarly journal which reports the outcomes of research into the impact of taking young offenders away to sea on a sail training ship. You may also find accounts written by enthusiasts for a particular activity (sailing) who write with great enthusiasm about the work they have done with particular groups of participants. You may also find the managers of a particular facility (in this case a sail training vessel) publishing information about their ship's benefits as a learning environment. All three publications may be of interest and have some value in your practice, but it is important to be able to discriminate between them, and to recognize the assumptions upon which they rest. Each publication is intended to do different work and is based upon different kinds of evidence to support its claims to truth. None of them, on its own, is a sufficient basis for deciding to adopt a new form of practice: the teacher must weigh the available information in the light of the particular needs of their learners, the learning outcomes which they wish to realize, and so on.

In analysing the role that learning environments play, careful investigation of built environments should prompt a deeper appreciation of teaching and learning in them and in virtual analogues. We shall consider three aspects of material and virtual domains: *structure*, *functionality* and *appearance*. These relate to some key questions about teaching, as shown in the box.

Aspect	Attributes	Relevance to teaching
Structure	What is special about this place? What is its purpose? Are there others like it?	What is the learning potential here?
Functionality	What is this structure used for? Who will I meet here?	What can I do here? How do I communicate with the people I meet?
Appearance	What does it look and sound like? Is it attractive as well as useful?	How do I feel about being here?

These three aspects are discussed in the following sections.

Built (real) environments

Structure

An expansion of provision in some of the formal educational sectors (for example, in higher education) has generated a widespread demand for new buildings. One such initiative was the development of a new library and resource centre (particularly for the use of undergraduate students) at the University of Sheffield, known as the Information Commons. (A virtual tour is available online, from Sheffield's website.) It won one of the regional Royal Institute of British Architects (RIBA) awards in 2008, and is a good example of the kind of building being commissioned to support and sustain greater variety in approaches to learning. When compared with a traditional university library, it is possible to see that changes of pedagogy and attitude to learners are realized in the building itself, as well as in the facilities that it provides. In some parts of the research student community in the city, it is known as 'the early learning centre', referencing a popular retailer of educational products for young children. This flippant name, itself used in good humour, indicates the sophistication of the relationship between the structure of learning environments and their reputational value, and the underlying (and perhaps healthy) scepticism about the extent to which changes are substantive or cosmetic.

The British Library is another example of a built learning environment that is structured to meet a particular purpose. A key design and pedagogic objective was widening access; it achieved its purpose so well (drawing in a remarkable community, including international scholars, local citizens pursuing projects of their own interest, professional writers, undergraduate students, and local school children doing projects) that public controversy arose in the national press in 2008 about the building's capacity to contain such diverse populations without degrading the quality of the experience within it. This incident illustrates not only how the structure of a learning environment professes its purpose, but also how the selection of a particular structure often represents compromises. These compromises may be apparent at the design and roll-out stage, or they may not manifest themselves until later.

Two other landmark buildings in London – University College Hospital's cruciform building in Gower Street, and Bankside Power Station (now Tate Modern) on the south bank of the river Thames – illustrate not only the potential for successful adaptation of environments to educational purposes, but also the limitations of this approach. These buildings have been (very effectively) refurbished to provide dedicated facilities for formal medical education and the housing, conservation and display of an eminent collection of modern art respectively. Nonetheless, while most of the learning which now takes place within them is moulded by the refurbishment (and the purposes which lay behind it), the original character of the building (embodied in the structural fabric which was not changed) continues to exert a subtle influence on activity. The dramatic context of Tate Modern's architecture, for example, obviously stimulates a certain range of approaches to the interpretation of the art hung within it. In the same way, adapting learning technologies or environments from one context to another may be very successful (as well as economically desirable) but we must not deny that it also has a tangible effect.

The structure of learning environments can have considerable impact on individuals, as well as at the grand scale, through their social implications (including differences in power). Learning environments have traditionally indicated clear territorial boundaries between teachers and learners. My first classroom as a school teacher (in 1974) arranged the (humble) pupils' desks in neat rows, and the (grand) teacher's desk on a raised platform facing them at the front. This elevated position improved surveillance (sometimes very usefully!) and indicated the prescribed social hierarchy. Rearranging the furniture for small group work was more or less impossible, and delivering teaching from anywhere other than the raised platform required the teacher to prowl up and down the rows, or stand at the back while the learners looked forward (both configurations also expressing the teacher's power and authority). The learning environment thus exerted a very strong pedagogic influence, despite my own preference for a more facilitative style.

In stark contrast, I also taught contemporary dance in the school assembly hall. This was a large, free-form space, an attribute essential for a field which is much less formal than classroom subjects. The relationship between teacher and learners is not so hierarchical, and the learning space is genuinely shared more flexibly. However, although the physical requirements were in principle entirely sufficient for expert performance, the implications of other aspects of its structure nonetheless made teaching within it difficult. The hall possessed a very high ceiling, below which a first-floor balcony provided access and egress to a series of classrooms. The head teacher's study was located nearby, as was the staff room. As a result, teaching was likely to be observed, without warning, by a wide range of people (including by our peers and superiors, both mine and the learners). The effect of this situation was entirely emotional (intellectually, I was confident in my teaching, and I worked hard to foster the learners' similar confidence in their performance) and yet it was undeniably real. Although entirely 'sufficient' for my teaching, it nonetheless required me to work much harder to overcome my feeling of continuous exposure and maintain my standards of work. I used to envy my colleagues who worked in parts of the building which seemed optimal to their fields (such as the art studio, which was in an isolated position on the top floor, and benefited from enormous amounts of natural light, privacy, space) but I also had to acknowledge that, until I was in a position to step into their shoes, there was a possibility that deficiencies existed there too of which I was not aware. It is very difficult for teachers to explain the qualities of learning environments which affect their teaching to anyone who is not a close colleague – and it is even harder to assess the point at which a disadvantage ceases to be a reasonable professional challenge to overcome and represents instead an obstacle to professionally competent practice.

The efficiency and confidence with which teachers and learners can relate to each other, and to the work of learning, is also influenced by the structure of the environment in which the learning is to take place. Residential courses offer intense, and sometimes prolonged, immersion in a particular physical environment and the society of those who are sharing the space. Short-term residential environments include conferences, activity centres, tours by performing artists and sports teams, field trips, sail training vessels, cultural or business exchange programmes, remedial boot camps, summer schools and retreats, and so on. Prison and university are examples of long-term residential learning environments. These experiences often exert a particularly powerful influence on learning and teaching. Reasons for this include the experience of displacement from one's usual environment and the consequences of adaptation, 'instant' membership of a new community, freedom from normal daily responsibilities, and the opportunity to be single-minded in the pursuit of learning. At the same time, the environment makes specific ethical and professional demands on teachers who work within it, and is in general much less forgiving. This form of teaching can be exhausting for all concerned, and particular care must be taken to protect participants from the consequences of their own vulnerabilities.

A related concept, the idea of going on retreat, is centuries old, and has been practised on different occasions by members of a wide range of cultures. The purpose of the exercise is to enable withdrawal from everyday life for a time of refreshment, productive activity, personal reflection, or spiritual and physical renewal. Participants may undertake some particular challenge while in retreat, or may seek to deny themselves the experiences and relationships which normally occupy them in order to prepare the mind for a new experience. It is hard to predict what will come to the surface, or even if there will be a recognizable outcome. Retreats are not excuses for self-indulgence or excess, and they can include periods of self-denial. Any adult learner may find it essential to withdraw into private space (physically or virtually) in order to concentrate upon their work without distraction. Interestingly, we can analyse it as a circumstance in which the learner, rather than the teacher, takes active control over their learning environment, and shapes it to their own purposes. As such, although it is generally not a model sustainable over a long period of time, it can be very effective.

Another consideration in examining the structure of learning environments is the idea of risk. Outdoor education provides opportunities to take part in challenging activities in a (more or less) natural environment.

This form of education can include an enormous range of activities: off-the-cuff examples include rock climbing, canoeing, sailing (dinghy and larger craft), orienteering, hill walking and trekking and scuba diving. There are many more. Each activity depends upon a unique physical relationship to the environment. Most are safety critical and so they demand engagement from learner and instructor in a wholehearted way. You cannot easily give half your attention to learning (or teaching) how to sail a boat or climb a rock face.

So much of the potential for good or ill associated with teaching is about power. Learning any new activity may be frightening. The sources of such fear include confrontation with one's own incompetence, fear of humiliation in front of others, anxiety about spending money, time and opportunity cost on an endeavour in which success is not guaranteed. In the context of most outdoor activities, we can add to this already unstable mix of fears the genuine risk of personal peril. Such risk is an essential element in the potency of the potential learning, and largely defines the outcome of the learning. When learning in the outdoors, participants thus become capable in a new way: they overcome one of the most basic fears, concern for personal safety. In this sense, the 'core' learning which occurs in this context does not concern the mechanics of sailing a boat or climbing a cliff (useful though these skills may be): rather, it is about developing the capacity to cope with the personal fears and the learning environment itself. Teachers of activities in high-risk environments have to develop an enhanced ability to make fine judgements about the scope and nature of challenge appropriate to each learner. In fact, this is the same judgement in kind made by all teachers, in almost all circumstances; the risk inherent in the learning environment, however, renders the ability of the teacher more transparent and the consequences of incompetence more immediately dangerous. Such judgement is not simply technical; it also requires an assessment of the learner's character, and especially the extent to which the learner tends towards overconfidence or a lack thereof. Teachers are constantly weighing in their mind the time to encourage the next step, the next risk, the next movement and when to build confidence through repetition of already acquired competence. They should never bully, humiliate or threaten learners. Many adults recall experiences of such behaviour and, even if they produced an apparent gain in the short term, rarely identify a sustained positive outcome. Conversely, those instructors who could live 'in the moment' with the learner, 'spot the wave', and move them on to the next experience of genuine success, achieved in their own way and at their own time, probably shared a lasting experience of real merit.

Functionality

Functionality in this context describes the teaching and learning activities for which the structure is best suited and the facilities it provides for the intended users. The environment may have positive attributes which provide opportunities for different users. I shall discuss some of those attributes commonly found in several different environments, starting with museums.

There are about 2500 museums and galleries throughout the UK, with varying functions. They enable collections of objects (anything from lawnmowers to fine art) to be stored, conserved and catalogued. These tasks are carried out because of the intrinsic value of the objects themselves and/or in order to make them accessible to visitors. Teaching and learning may be among the uses made of such collections. Indeed, members of the Campaign for Learning through Museums and Galleries (CLMG), a think-tank, suggest that learning may be *the* most important reason for the existence of museums and galleries. When a group of policy and opinion formers came together in 2003 to debate the question 'What are museums for?', they reached this conclusion:

> What came out of all the debate was a new way of thinking about museums' role in society – their influence on learning, on mental health, on democracy, on culture itself – not from an instrumental point of view (that would mean hitching museums to every policy bandwagon with money on it), but from the point of view of the vital things in life they can do better than anyone else or that only museums can do.
>
> (CLMG, reported on its website, www.clmg.org.uk)

The Museums, Libraries and Archives Council is the UK government body which sponsors the Inspiring Learning for All project. It explored the means by which the people who work in museums and galleries could develop learning 'outputs' for themselves. This project positions the actualization of the learning potential of the museum or gallery as a major management responsibility. Improved access to museums and their collections will enable them to begin to exploit their potential. Access in this context means more than simply making the building easier to get into and navigate around (although huge improvements have been made in such basic attributes of a learning environment). The term recognizes that the whole fabric of the organization needed to build confidence of visitors in their ability to engage with the objects on show. (The British Library, which we have already discussed, is an excellent example.) A constructivist approach to knowledge creation was adopted as paradigmatic (i.e. as a standard assumption), so there was considerable emphasis on generating opportunity for interaction with the objects to foster learning. Curators and designers were encouraged to develop displays and materials with potential for activity in contrast with the somewhat passive experience of disinterested contemplation which might previously have characterized the stance of the typical museum or gallery visitor.

There is an opportunity and a risk associated with this approach. The benefit of working in this way is that the local experts were challenged to explore the learning potential of their own buildings and collections to develop their function as sources of learning for all kinds of visitors. Many museums and galleries (local and national) conducted their own research and determined an approach based upon that study. It is highly likely that the approach they adopt will be carried through because it was determined locally within a national framework. There is less risk of the 'not invented here' resistance to implementation which has characterized other national initiatives based upon the outcomes of a geographically or culturally distant pilot. It is likely that by undertaking this work the managers of museums and galleries will identify many of the institutionally embedded economic, practical, organizational and attitudinal barriers to learning, as well as the physical ones. They may even be able to take action to remove them. They will be able to 'pick the ripe fruit off the low branches' of the new learning opportunity harvest. This is certainly to be welcomed. However, there is a risk that the depth of understanding of pedagogic issues (such as the appreciation of the emotional factors which inhibit learning, and remain hidden from a predominantly cognitive analysis), which is the domain of professional teachers, will be missing from this approach. Even where learning potential is abundant, it can take the skill of a teacher to ignite the mental touch-paper before such potential is realized. Genuine partnerships between museum staff and professional teachers will actualize the potential for active learning in libraries, archives museums and galleries more fully. We began this chapter on this very premise: the importance of a balanced relationship between teachers and other technical experts. In this context, they are museum staff; in the context of a virtual learning environment, they might be learning technologists. Meaningful adaptation or development of the functions of a learning environment, perhaps even more than its structure (which may or may not be a given, and can be worked around) or appearance (which may be 'spun'), requires the collaboration of the two.

'Precision-engineered' teaching spaces also represent a useful example to consider. One example is the learning lab. or language lab., normally a purpose-built facility with relatively high specifications, refined by the combined experience of many teachers in relevant specialisms. It may have a wide range of functions from which an individual teacher has considerable freedom to select for a specific group of learners. (At the same time, its structure often severely constrains other kinds of activities which the teacher might have chosen to include.) It generally seeks to exclude distraction, and focus on optimizing conditions for the intended learning. Other examples of such tailored spaces might include theatres, dance studios (but not assembly halls!), music practice rooms, modern gymnasiums, swimming pools, art studios, potteries, audio and film editing suites, and so on. In other words, these environments are tailored to enable the frequent repetition of practice which is associated with mastery of a single art or craft. They are often costly to resource, intensively used, and (at best) have competent teachers on hand to encourage, guide and instruct the development of masterly technique or application. Spaces of this sort are most appropriate for the involvement of 'pure' technical experts in the teaching process, and (when properly used) they may also represent an ideal forum for situated learning. At the same time, except for the most single-minded of learners, the space or the kit alone rarely generates learning. It may appear intimidating or baffling and even once such uncertainty is overcome, in the course of venturing outside the space to perform their work in a real-life context, learners may be in need of the full range of feedback from teachers, not just technical evaluation. It is worth noting that the great cost of these facilities may lead (unhelpfully, although understandably) to institutional pressure to use them for purposes for which they are not suited (or for learners who are not motivated to work in such environments). This can be very problematic, and easily provokes conflict between 'generic' teachers, who are required to use the space for other purposes, and the primary stakeholders of the space in its intended context.

Most new learning and teaching spaces in formal learning environments are now designed with at least some sense of the range of social interactions which learning might require. Constructivist perspectives on learning have influenced practice to a sufficient extent that designers anticipate that learners will need to be able to interact with each other, and with their teachers, in different ways. Large group teaching in lecture theatres (or their equivalent) may now benefit from, for example, infra-red personal response systems to aid communication. This technology enables participants to answer questions, record votes and so on. The system should enable each participant to see if their response has been recorded as well as viewing the aggregated results as a graph on a screen. Individuals will know immediately if they agree or disagree with their peers on questions designed to test knowledge. Tutor and students know how the learning is progressing and which material may need to be covered again in a different way or if more opportunities are needed for practice. The questions must be carefully worded and the activities properly integrated into the learning session but, when well used, this technology has the potential to be a really useful aid. One good example of their use is with large groups of students who have recently completed clinical rotations. They are able to have some basic aspects of their recent learning tested, and have the opportunity to record their views on the quality of the placement they undertook. The system may not promote particularly subtle responses but it will identify which students need to be followed up by tutors.

Appearance

First impressions are important. The appearance of a learning space needs to encourage potential learners to enter and spend time within it, preferably within the 'right' frame of mind. The British Library, already discussed, provides an excellent example. Visitors are drawn into the building through an impressive gateway and across a spacious, land-scaped courtyard. Just inside the library building, the information desk is clearly visible at ground level, while stairs, ramps and escalators lead down to cloakrooms and up towards the reading rooms, cafés and private study spaces. The public has free access to a book and gift shop and exhibi-tion spaces. Anyone can enjoy it as a place for calm relaxation, located just off one of London's busiest streets, and/or as the access point to one of the world's most prestigious collections of books and publications. I very much enjoy taking MA students there in order to inspire them as they start work on dissertations: a student from China was speechless as he began to get to know the building, received a reader's pass and entered the humanities reading room. He found it hard to believe that such a resource was freely available to students like him.

Obviously, we cannot all benefit from world-class architecture to augment our teaching. However, the appearance of a learning environ-ment is the variable most easily altered, requiring a little effort and some thought. Key practical considerations for enhancing the appearance of any physical learning environment are largely common-sense. When a space is welcoming and comfortable, people are likely to be willing to spend more time in it, and to be less distracted. Accordingly, heating and ventilation should be efficient while unobtrusive. Natural daylight is valued whenever possible, and artificial lighting design needs to reduce glare while providing sufficient illumination for print or screen media to be read easily. Furniture may be built into the space (as in many lecture theatres) or movable. If there is discretion about the placement of furniture, thought should be given to its appearance as well as its func-tionality: inappropriate seating encouragements can serve to distract, or even alter the way participants feel about themselves or others.

Litter and general mess make any space look and feel much worse. Some teaching spaces receive very heavy use and by the end of a day they are exhausted. Ideally, ensure you arrive at least five minutes before your participants in order to take control of the space. If necessary, tidy up the furniture, remove litter, clean the white board or chalk board if there is one, improve the ventilation and provide tangible evidence of welcome. If you cannot get there first (or even when you do), encourage the learners to share responsibility for this housekeeping, which is to everyone's benefit.

Those who are responsible for the maintenance and cleaning of teaching environments may impose rules which are intended to help them to ensure that the space is fit for purpose within the constraints on their budgets (for example rules which say 'Don't move the furniture', 'Don't attach material to the walls' and so on). On occasion, teachers may have to seek a more suitable space for teaching, or adapt the way essential activities are undertaken to ensure the space is left in good condition for those who follow. When conditions are not ideal, teachers can do a lot to ameliorate the disadvantages associated with working in those surroundings. However, it is also worth noting here that there are occasions when teachers reflecting on a session which did not go as well as they had hoped are inclined to blame themselves or the learners. It is always appropriate to consider too if the conditions (physical environment, time of day, weather or previous activity undertaken by the learners for example) also had an impact. Patterns can emerge. Sometimes teachers must work very hard to counter the negative impact of the wider environment, itself potentially beyond their direct control. Where this is suspected, it may be possible to explore the issue with some or all of the learners to see if they are also aware of the pattern. Once identified, teacher and learners can work together to overcome the problem.

It may always remain impossible to provide the ideal environment, perhaps most frequently because the perfect conditions may be too expensive for the budget available to a particular course. Such an assumption should not always go unchallenged, however. Many teachers, particularly those early in their careers, may accept that the conditions within which they and their participants are expected to work cannot be changed. Nonetheless, where the environment provided is frequently inappropriate, it is not unreasonable to enquire into the underlying reasons, if any, and when some improvement might be reasonably anticipated. Teachers have a responsibility for the care and wellbeing of the learners entrusted to them. That may mean representing their interests to those in authority. As people get older, attention to detail on the basic standards becomes even more important. Similarly, if learners have specific disabilities, every effort should be made to ensure that their needs are met.

E-learning

Virtual learning environments (VLEs) can appear to liberate learners and teachers from the constraints of the physical environment. In truth, however, they merely distribute the environment across time and space: although the interaction between teacher and learner, learner and learner, or learner and material may become 'virtual', participants interface with the process in a physical context which will itself exercise an effect upon their practice. In analysing the role and utility of VLEs, we should be wary of any rhetoric that seeks to deny their physical reality. In practical terms, use of VLEs merely swaps one configuration of the physical learning environment for another. There are advantages and disadvantages to both models. Use of VLEs may be particularly attractive to institutions as a relatively small investment in their creation may free up large amounts of physical resources. The learner is often expected to rely on their own facilities (accessing the VLE remotely, via their own computer, from their own home), permitting the institution to draw-down its provision. Once started, this can become an escalating trend: the more physical provision is reduced, the greater the incentive there is to the learner not to compete for the limited common facilities but to rely upon their own. For obvious reasons, although institutional needs for economy are understandable, there are serious drawbacks to this sort of 'rationalization'. VLEs may also offer learners the benefit of convenience, enabling 24-hour access to learning which may be useful to part-time professional learners, even if it is not entirely appropriate to a healthy work–life balance. It is also worth remembering that many adult learners already spend many hours each day working at a computer: repetitive strain injury, lower back pain, headaches and weight gain can all arise from spending too much time seated and working with C&IT. This is a health and safety consideration which is often overlooked.

Structure

Teachers may be in a position to select between options when considering the use of technology to support their teaching, or they may be required to use particular approaches which have been commissioned at institutional or departmental levels. Degrees of autonomy in this area will vary considerably. Access to dedicated VLE software, such as Moodle, webCT and Blackboard, generally requires institutional engagement.

Teachers with responsibility for course design or management should retain the discretion, however, to select the particular 'blend' of real and virtual learning environment(s) in the interests of the learners and the learning process. The proportion of face-to-face teaching to virtual engagement is particularly important in structuring the learning environment which the learner perceives as a whole. Although sole reliance upon one or the other is possible, many teachers find that a combination is more effective, all other circumstances being equal. Certainly, there is informal evidence to suggest that the degree to which learners happily engage with VLEs is closely related to a blended approach; despite the rhetoric that adult learners value the opportunity to get 'off the leash', to set their own pace and timetable for learning, and to be independent, the enthusiasm of learners' engagement with virtual learning seems to be affected by the extent to which it is integrated with 'real' teaching. One (at least partial) explanation may be that the opportunity for real teaching to engage with the many non-cognitive aspects of the learning process (see Chapter 5) leads to a more speedy breakdown of the natural social barriers that initially exist between participants. Interactivity by virtual means may rise sharply when there is a more human context to the identities of those involved.

In this context, the rise of online 'virtual worlds' such as Second Life represents an interesting development. Through means of an 'avatar' (a customizable three-dimensional graphic representation of an individual), participants may communicate with other people, access information and material, and generally interact in a form which is mediated by a graphic (almost cartoonish) representation of 'real life'. This software is, in essence, a giant computer game, simulating the physical world. At least for the enthusiasts, this nod towards the real experience confers some of the benefits upon a virtual interaction that they would gain from meeting in the real world. There is a 'face' to put to a name – even if the face is entirely constructed at the user's whim, rather than on the basis of 'objective' reality. Sceptics may view this initiative as smoke and mirrors; watching representations of people sitting around an open fire under a dark sky is not, for them, the same as actually doing it. Nonetheless, a number of educational institutions are exploring the possible applications of this type of virtual forum: in the UK, the Open University's 'Schome' project (a contraction of 'School' and 'Home') has begun to explore the potential of Second Life for the education of children and adults. An interesting, if somewhat ambitious, website is available, citing a growing list of published work which has come out of this development.

Despite likely institutional support for one VLE system over another, teachers may also possess the core choice to use virtual technologies in a dispersed or integrated way. The dispersed approach ((for example, communicating via email, distributing content through (public or private) standard 'read-only' web pages, and reflecting upon taught sessions via 'wiki' (i.e. user editable) web pages) offers great flexibility but has the potential drawback of appearing complicated and/or confused. Dedicated VLE systems integrate many functions into a coherent whole but, in so doing, may increase participants' dependence upon the support of technical experts or access to further training. The dispersed approach tends to support an emphasis on 'real' teaching and, by use of off-the-shelf technologies with which participants are likely to be familiar from their daily lives, simplifies the questions of functionality and appearance. The integrated approach is likely to be more appropriate where the teacher anticipates significant collaborative work to be undertaken online but requires a correspondingly greater degree of preparation and thought.

Functionality

The functionality of virtual learning environments is perhaps one of the most controversial issues. Western society is already well acquainted with the benefits and frustrations of the information revolution, and most users can draw on direct personal experience of when 'the system' will or will not do what they want it to do. It is important to note, therefore, that individual attitudes to C&IT do not, in most cases, start from a blank canvas; individual engagement draws upon a wealth of prior experience, which may be positive or negative.

It is also true that, whatever the circumstances of the teaching and learning process, essentially the same core functions will need to be performed. These can be effectively carried out within either a virtual or material learning environment, although there are implications of convenience, cost, and professional choice in determining the best way to do this.

Teachers and technologists have worked together in the design of VLEs but they are still not without some limitations. At worst, e-learning packages have the capacity to do all sorts of things the teacher doesn't want the students to be able (or required) to do while they fail to deliver the actions or activities which are pedagogically desirable. VLE functionality is both generally limited to a discrete list permitted by the architecture of the software and made fully explicit to participants. Expectations that teaching and learning will be managed in a particular way can thus be raised by the apparent existence of available functions. This can load cost (in terms of time) onto a programme for some or all participants, including the teachers, and may encourage some dialogue between learner and teacher over method which tends not to occur when the question of functionality is implicit. Over time, it may also lead towards a kind of homogeneity as all teaching converges around the specifications built into the structure and functionality of the package. At best, VLEs enable an integrated approach to the recruitment, administration, content delivery, activity management and assessment of adult learning. They can aid efficiency and help to assure quality when large numbers of participants are going to take a relatively stable course taught by an individual or a group of teachers on several occasions. Under these conditions, the generally high initial investment of time and resource in setting up the VLE will secure a good return in the meeting of pre-specified learning outcomes.

The discipline required to produce high quality online material is itself an important reminder of the value to be found in learning from each other's practice. Whether one intends to deliver teaching via the Internet, as hard copy, or face-to-face, there are occasions when the planning and attention to detail which is essential for excellence in e-learning can be seen as a good example for all teachers.

Gilly Salmon's work (see e.g. Salmon 2002) is well known for its rigour in combination with a practical and accessible approach. She has written on the development of what she describes as 'e-tivities'. Salmon has generated a five-stage model for the running of asynchronous plenary sessions which relates in substance to a number of the aspects of teaching which this book introduces. Her model describes:

- Access and motivation
- Online socialization
- Information exchange
- Knowledge construction
- Development.

Whatever the blend of physical and virtual learning adopted, teachers guide and support learners in the progression through these stages by some mix of direct contact, design and delivery of purposeful, content-related activities and by facilitating peer interaction. The diagram Salmon uses to express this progression in the online context also indicates the mix of technical support and e-moderating that may be required. Moderation is the term used to describe the interventions made by the person responsible for the success of the activity: if the online engagement is about learning then the moderator may be fulfilling some of (but not necessarily all) the functions of a teacher. Moderation substantially improves the potential success of e-learning. Without it very few participants are sufficiently motivated to engage fully and sustain such engagement over time.

The principal functional benefit of virtual learning via the Internet is the possibility for distant participation in synchronous and asynchronous tasks in collaboration with peers and tutors. I am enthusiastic about the rich potential this approach has to offer. At the same time, there are concerns about the additional demand on teacher time it can represent. This 'overhead' of time has two elements. The first is the time taken to plan and design the teaching so that it makes the best use of the functionality available from the VLE. This may be extensive but it can, at least theoretically, be planned and the cost estimated. The second is more difficult since it concerns the expectations of the learners. Managing learner expectations is an important aspect of all adult teaching: they are often varied and unpredictable. Technology which offers the potential for interactivity (whether via simple e-mail contact, a contact 'phone number or the use of a sophisticated VLE) can encourage participants to expect immediate 24/7 access to their tutors throughout the year. In my own practice, I have also noticed an increase in the expectations of adult learners for material and staff time before a course starts and for it to continue once it has finished. In other words, a significant issue for the teachers of adults is the management of boundaries and the negotiation of legitimate expectations. While considerable sums of money have gone into developing the technologies to support e-learning, very little is available to research or implement evaluation of the true cost to teachers of introducing and sustaining teaching in this way. It is also interesting to note that research which compares the return on investment in C&IT with comparable sums spent on increasing time available to teachers for preparation, feedback or tutoring, for example, remains to be done.

A significant additional functional aspect of VLEs, which is more or less unique, is the possibility that they offer for surveillance of learners and teachers. Accessing any given function within a VLE, undertaking any task, reading any material, may be logged, the time and date recorded, and even a rough estimate of location made. This raises questions from a variety of perspectives about the uses to which this information may be acceptably put. These are briefly introduced later. Identifying this group of issues is not intended to provoke alarm: much of VLEs' potential is put to benign use. It is an ethical responsibility of the teacher, however, to be thoroughly aware of the potential for misuse, conflict of interest, and loss of confidence in the basis of teacher–learner relationship. This task becomes more complex in contemporary blended environments. Teachers need to combine a thorough understanding of relevant data protection and freedom of information legislation with a carefully worked-through (and transparent) ethical position.

In the pedagogic context, a common task for learners may be the writing of a reflective journal. When assessed, this work is taken at face value, and analysed for evidence of the underlying thought processes, their connection to the experiences of the author, and so on. The extent to which the journal is or is not a 'constructed' account is not made clear to the assessor. Were the same task to be transferred to a VLE, however, a reflective 'blog' would contain the same content, but each entry would be identifiable to a time and date, and the editing history would (in principle) be accessible. Would it change the assessor's judgement of the work were they to realize that the journal was, in fact, synoptically written at the end of the period to which it related, rather than day-by-day? Would it change their mind if the original journal was radically revised at the last minute? What if the last draft was less good than the original? Or vice versa? These sorts of insights into time management, and the process underlying the production of work, may introduce individual learning styles and practices into assessment in an overt way. Of itself not disastrous, it will however require a teacher who is conscious of their own preferences – and the fact that they are preferences, not 'right' or 'wrong' approaches – and potentially clear recognition in assessment criteria.

In the context of performance evaluation, the centralizing of data which VLEs encourage raises the possibility that teaching quality may be evaluated by the institution by reference to the number of online interventions made, their frequency, the lapse of time between question and answer, and so on. Such a quantifiable metric may be very attractive for audit purposes, but has obvious shortcomings as a holistic review of teaching activity.

The surveillance capacity means that, for the first time, teachers could practicably require learners to prove that they spent a certain amount of time on a given task, or require learners to continue to engage with the learning project in the course of their daily lives (through remote access of blogs, for example, or even Twitter posts via mobile phone). More complicated still, what if the learner is not paying their own course fees, but their employer? Traditional conceptions of the professional relationship indicate that the professional serves the interests of the fee-payer; traditional conceptions of the caring relationship indicate that the professional owes a duty of care to their 'patient', who may or may not pay. Which paradigm applies where, as many do, a learner has a financial sponsor? If an employer, for example, wishes to be informed of the time an individual spends actively 'learning', how should the teacher respond? As a general rule, increased access to personal data requires a clearer understanding of ethical obligations, and a procedure for transparently and appropriately reconciling conflicts of interest.

Appearance

Considerations of appearance in relation to e-learning highlight some interesting interrelated elements, such as design, maintenance and compatibility, and the interpretation of textual material and instructions (an issue more commonly associated with written forms of assessment, for example, rather than the learning environment itself). There is an obvious concern with making the virtual environment attractive and user-friendly. The appearance and content of individual VLE 'pages' need to ensure that learners, particularly at the start of a course, do not find themselves disorientated and unable to navigate their way around the site. Sometimes very attractive pages may be painfully slow to load, or may even cause the computer to crash if accessed through older versions of software. Alternatively, learners may experience less dramatic problems, and merely find directions for use hard to follow, preventing them from getting started. Just as people entering a new physical environment may be nervous about their ability to cope, or have doubts about whether they 'belong', entering a virtual space may similarly generate considerable anxiety for some. Moreover, although expertise in the virtual world permits communication and collaboration, initial entry is inevitably an individual (and potentially isolating) experience, unless it is facilitated in a 'real' context in some manner. It may be very hard for those who are comfortable with C&IT to recall how it feels to be a newcomer, in the same way that it may be difficult for experienced drivers to remember what it was like before they passed their test. In the context of material learning environments, teachers can at least tap the relatively common human experience of apprehension on entering a new social context to inform their practice. With technology, given that the interface for one programme is frequently based on similar logic to another, this sense of disorientation is thus much less usual once basic competence has been achieved. Care should be taken not to discount it all together.

Time taken to customize (or 'decorate') a VLE so that it is distinctive, welcoming and recognizable to participants seems a good investment. However, the evidence base for this assumption is mixed. Some small-scale local experimentation with the provision of resources located in a specially designed Moodle site indicates that, even when considerable time and expense is put into ensuring that the site has been carefully tailored to a particular course, looks attractive and recognizable, the content relevant and up to date, many participants in a course declined to use it. The course team concerned has experimented with many ways of introducing the site, and the materials contained within it, to participants in the face-to-face element of the course. They encouraged participants to use it for communication, content retrieval and the independent recording of progress. It has still not yet proved successful, however. In this particular context, it looks as if there has been no added value from access to the Moodle compared with the earlier practice of giving participants hard copies of all resources in a workshop pack. The only clearly identifiable benefit in this instance was the reduced cost of printing material, and the greater ease of updating for tutors.

This example illustrates some of the difficulties of innovation in teaching and learning. Evidently, the use of the VLE in the circumstances described earlier has not been an unparalleled success; at the same time, other courses have successfully blended virtual and real learning environments. It is difficult to isolate the variable(s) which affect or control the outcomes. Many of the students whom I encounter have a science-based background. They are often surprised by the scarcity of research into educational innovation; they recognize the context as being akin to that of a clinical trial. Certainly, it would be fascinating to experiment along these lines, for example by giving one group of participants hard copies of the resources, another group just access to Moodle, and a third group both. Unfortunately, the ethical tradition and practices that permit this form of experimentation in a clinical context does not really do so for teaching and learning. Teachers are obliged to prioritize the interests of the learning process and learners, and therefore cannot arbitrarily refuse access to certain materials to some learners but not others. Learners whose performance was impaired, and thus suffered loss of reputation, loss of benefit and so on, might be justifiably angry. At the same time, simulations (like model juries) are expensive to set up and hard to verify: it is almost impossible to draw firm conclusions from them which fully represent the complexity of real life.

Unlike the arrangement of most physical learning environments, teachers may find themselves unable to influence the presentation of the virtual environment in which they work, either because it is 'owned' by others or because they lack the time or ability to do so themselves. This can be a cause of discomfort in itself, as management of the learning environment is one of the chief professional competences of the teacher. Work in partnership with learning technologists may remedy the problems posed by lack of ability – and itself represents valuable professional development for the teacher, who cannot really afford to be ill-informed of the basics of this area. It is much more problematic when time or property interests restrain the teacher's action. It is reasonably common for teachers to feel pressure to change their preferred teaching style to make it more cost-efficient, more accessible to new markets, to include under-represented groups, to minimize contact time, to increase group size, to standardize it with the approaches of other colleagues, and so on. Although learning might ideally be informed only by academic considerations, it is situated in the real world, with all the tensions that ensue. It is, however, the teacher's professional responsibility to make sound judgements about the extent to which compliance with institutional concerns of the nature we have described represents a permissible or impermissible interference with the interests of the learner and the learning process. Teachers need to have the courage to engage with colleagues from varied backgrounds to resolve problems as they arise – and need to be clear about both their pedagogy and the capacities of the technology in order to judge their interventions carefully.

Conclusion

Constructivist theories of learning, although significant in many aspects of adult teaching and learning, do not have to decentre the teacher from the teaching and learning process. Exploration of the idea of learning environments provides an excellent model for demonstrating that constructivist approaches are most effectively consummated when facilitated by a relevant professional.

Consideration of learning environments also foregrounds issues which relate to all aspects of teaching practice. In a very real way, technological development, and the specialization of certain environments, raises the question of the teacher's agency, and the extent of their professional stake in control of the learning context. It highlights their need to work collaboratively with professionals from other fields, and to reflect upon their own core competences, values and areas in which they make constructive contributions. The idea of 'blended' teaching is helpful in contradicting a monolithic analysis of teaching practice, and advancing the teacher's identity as pedagogic expert practitioner (capable of accurate diagnosis of the needs of the learner and learning process, and selecting appropriate means and methods as a result). The very diversity of learning environments also illustrates the breadth of contexts of adult learning, and the varying interests for which it must cater.

3   Recognizing effective teachers: Professional identity, power and evaluation

You may be reading this book because you want to become a better teacher, or because you are encouraging others in the improvement of their practice. A growing number of colleagues work in colleges and universities training and developing students early in their careers as teachers of adults. Similarly, the MA students with whom I work the most are mid-career professionals who never set out to become teachers. They lead, mediate, inspire and assess adult learning in their workplaces and communities. As they look for ways to do this more effectively, they question much that I take for granted. Such questioning, especially of my assumptions about effective teaching, is a good place to begin this chapter.

As an experienced teacher myself, every time my students ask why I choose to do one thing rather than another, I have to consider the possibility that it may be because it is the easier, safer or cheaper option, rather than the one which will do the most to promote learning. Teachers are human too, and are subject to the competing pressures of all professional people. Effective teaching does not rule such pragmatism out of order but it does presume that, while necessary at times, it may not be sufficient in the long run. Excellent teaching may be thrifty but never parsimonious. Making judgements about what constitutes good teaching practice, or even merely 'acceptable', is one of the hardest things to do, especially as it may be undertaken by those who are not teachers themselves.

This chapter is an opportunity to explore what it means to be a teacher of adults in the twenty-first century. In this safe space, we are free to wonder about ourselves; what we have in common and how we are diverse. We shall ask how much personal freedom and responsibility we have and we shall try to discern how the interplay between our actions and the systems in which we work determines the progress of the learners who entrust their learning to us. We shall explore the interactions which together make up the recognition of effective teaching, think about the factors which shape our careers, qualify us for awards and feel professional satisfaction with our own performance.

Rather like an onion, the recognition of effective teaching is an idea wrapped in layers of meaning. As we peel the layers away, you should begin to feel more confident in your ability to:

- Reflect critically and creatively on your own performance as teachers
- Reconcile competing demands from learners and other stakeholders to determine priorities for learning and teaching
- Prepare learners to make considered and responsible judgements on the teaching which they experience
- Provide evidence of your own competence as teachers
- Celebrate the unexpected outcomes of teaching.

Let us begin by considering the notion of 'recognition' as it applies to teaching, and looking at the way the changing organizational context in which most of us work has an impact on what counts as effective teaching. Beyond that, we shall explore the way our peers and students share responsibility in recognizing effective teaching. Finally, we shall discuss how we see ourselves and gather, interpret and represent evidence of our own competence.

In many sectors, evidence-based assertions of teaching standards have recently become much more important, and this seems unlikely to change in the foreseeable future. We are responsible for developing a robust sense of professional identity. It defines who we are as teachers, while we engage in dialogue with learners, colleagues, sponsors and society as a whole. Teachers who are true to themselves and have confidence in the value of their calling have always been most likely to inspire confidence in their learners. This is no longer enough. Now, most of us also have to provide evidence of that which was formerly just between teacher and learner for managers, sponsors and regulators. How we approach this is an important professional concern. If the burden weighs heavily, we shall be exhausted by anxiety about whether we are good enough. If we try to disregard it altogether, we run the risk of being unaware of our own need for improvement, or our work remains undervalued and insignificant. Our professional responsibility is to ourselves and each other in finding a sustainable, balanced approach.

This chapter may all sound rather theoretical. However, it is significant for practice in two ways. First, as one might expect, it introduces some models for teachers to manage the recognition of teaching, important for the purposes of evaluating performance and professional development. Second, the chapter also seeks to give a framework for the teacher to interpret (and cope with) the *feeling* of having their work scrutinized. Many teachers, along with other public and voluntary sector workers, report dissatisfaction at 'not getting the respect they deserve'. This is, in substantial part, a direct consequence of the subtleties of the recognition process, and the shifting power relations of those who govern it. An understanding of these subtleties may at least help to relieve some of the stress felt by teachers, and perhaps permit the tailoring of behaviour to meet the needs of particular situations.

What do we mean by 'recognition'?

The *Oxford English Dictionary* offers a multilayered definition of the meaning of 'recognition' which includes the following:

> 4. The action of acknowledging as true, valid, or entitled to consideration; formal acknowledgement as conveying approval or sanction of something; hence, notice or attention accorded to a thing or person . . .

> 7. The action or fact of perceiving that something, person, etc, is the same as one previously known; the mental process of identifying what has been known before; the fact of being thus known or identified.

At heart, the term depends on the core ideas of *identification* and *acknowledgement of merit*. There is an implied link between the value of the action and the status of the actor, which may be enhanced (or degraded) by consequent changes in title, responsibilities and privileges.

When considering how we recognize teaching, we are thus faced with the following issues:

- How do we identify the criteria by which we recognize good teaching: what does good teaching look like?
- How do we identify fair, appropriate and transparent processes by which we can recognize good teaching practice by particular teachers, teams or agencies?
- How do we identify the people or agencies competent to undertake this process? This may include an acknowledgement that this competence is distributed between various stakeholders on the basis of their own interest, or the obligation of accountability owed in a democratic society.
- How do we translate an act of recognition into a meaningful outcome?

Acknowledging the big picture

Cullen et al. (2002), in their review of pedagogic research, indicate that there is some confusion associated with varied understandings of what constitute 'proximal' and 'distal' factors. For ease of understanding here, I am going to refer to proximal factors as those elements more closely controlled by teachers and learners in the shared space inhabited by their learning, while distal factors acknowledge the broader context, considering the influences and interests of larger organizations or groups and indeed society in general.

In discussing ideas of recognition and teaching quality, there may be a certain inclination to focus on proximal factors: what individual teachers do in the classroom, how and why; or, at most, what teams of teachers do collectively (identified as particular departments, faculties, colleges and so on). Terms like 'evaluation', 'audit', 'review', for example, rather contribute to this notion, albeit unavoidably. There is a frequent sense that 'the quality agenda' is about control, standardizing individual performances to an acceptable average. However, although quality assurance is undoubtedly important, it is a much narrower notion than that of recognizing effective teaching generally, which logically should entail implications for quality enhancement. Consideration of both the proximal *and* distal levels is a helpful corrective. First, it highlights that factors affecting teaching quality extend far outside the particular classroom, and into the broader institution and society as a whole. Many quality assurance processes take account of this to a certain extent, but often only to the limits of relevant administrative or procedural requirement. As teaching professionals, interested in the recognition of effective teaching for its own sake, our analysis may be different in its scope. Second, it highlights the widely varying levels at which recognition takes place.

At the very least, the recognition of effective teaching is important in at least five contexts. The following list introduces these contexts, and illustrates how the concerns of individuals working in each may vary.

The macro-level: government or wide-scale policy-makers

- How do those responsible for education and training policy set targets?
- How do they know when those targets have been met?
- How do they allocate resources for those targets?
- How is the *responsible* use of those resources analysed?
- How is the *effective* use of those resources analysed? (This may not be the same thing.)
- How do they manage systems for the fair and effective conduct of these analyses?

The mid-level: a professional or quality assurance body

- How are they structured to meet their mission?
- When do they claim success? How do they identify it?

- Where do they source their staff?
- How do they educate or train their staff to carry out their mission?
- How do they manage their members?
- What standards do they ask their members to meet?
- How do they choose to express these standards?
- What disciplinary sanctions might they impose upon their members, if any?
- What 'pull' to compliance do they exert?

The mid-level: an institution

- How do they assess success or failure in meeting the goals they have been set by society?
- How do they set their own internal targets?
- How do they allocate internal resources for those targets?
- How is the *responsible* use of those resources analysed?
- How is the *effective* use of those resources analysed? (This may not be the same thing . . .)
- How do they manage systems for the fair and effective conduct of these analyses?
- How do they manage their staff effectively, recognizing and rewarding 'achievement' and encouraging improvement and personal development?

The micro-level: a teacher

- How did they perform, in a given teaching scenario?
- How might they improve their teaching? What does 'better' teaching look like?
- Is there an incentive or cost to doing so? Do they care?
- How do they identify relevant CPD opportunities?
- How do they recognize a colleague or peer from whom they can learn?
- How do they find an appropriate mentor, coach, teacher or confidant?
- How do they identify and manage risk?

The micro-level: a learner

- How do they evaluate their performance as learner (which requires an assessment of the relative contribution of their teacher)?

- How do they recognize a good teacher?
- How do they recognize a 'favourite' teacher?
- How do they assess their own vocation or inspiration for a particular field (discounting the personal charisma – or otherwise – of relevant teachers)?
- How do they identify risk and seek help from other sources if required?

Given that all of the questions identified above potentially relate to the recognition of effective teaching, it is clear that engagement with this topic is both important and in need of something more than a 'tick box' approach.

It is also clear that the type of evaluation which each context needs may vary, according to the different purpose of those who work within it. The kind of data which an individual learner or teacher may require is likely to be very different from the kind of data that a civil servant with responsibility for national education policy may require. The distinct variation in power and influence between the five groups of stakeholders should alert us to the possibility that the needs of one group may be 'drowned out' (at least in the policy arena) by the needs of another.

The changing purposes of teaching and learning

One of the big questions underlying this chapter is simply 'What is adult learning for?' If we are interested in exploring what it may look like, this question cannot be avoided. Again, there is no easy answer, not least because since the 1950s, adult learning has come into its own. As such, its purposes are varied, and changing as fast as modern society. It is worth taking a little time to look at some of the ways in which this change might have occurred and how it impacts on the recognition of effective teaching.

In the UK and Europe (as well as Australia, the Americas and some parts of Asia and Africa), 'change' has tended to be a policy goal in and of itself since at least the 1980s. Educational systems which had enjoyed considerable stability were, and are, required to modernize.

In England, adult learning policy has had a much higher public profile since about 1990, driving changes to funding regimes and the regulation of practice. These initiatives were not theory-led, but ideologically loaded, instrumental responses to perceived geopolitical, socio-economic, technological and demographic trends. Rising concern with phenomena such as the post-industrial society, the knowledge economy, the digital or information age and the ageing population seemed (reasonably) to demand a response of this sort (see Chapter 6). At the same time, it is hard to deny that the implications of this quiet revolution were not fully thought through, and that the successful implementation of some of the policy ideals remains a work in progress. As teachers, although we are in part responsible to society, we should not be uncritical of, much less blind to, the power or effect of these influences. We have a professional duty to shape our own practice to new policy requirement – but informed by our own, expert understanding of the theoretical and practical issues involved.

Unfortunately, the higher profile given to adult learning was not always matched by an enhanced understanding of it. Policy analysts had proposed a causal link between participation in lifelong learning and the prosperity of post-industrial economies. The lure of an economic return (on a societal level, rather than for particular individuals) served to push adult teaching and learning up the political agenda yet simultaneously narrowed the context in which it was considered. Private, voluntary and personally fulfilling motivations for learning in adult life were (at the time) substantially marginalized by significant investment in (or reallocation of other funds to) training and development which met the needs of the labour market, in public and private sectors. This initiative was exemplified in England by the (rather unfortunately named) 'PICKUP' initiative, funding further and higher education to develop short courses for professional, industrial and commercial knowledge updating in the early 1990s. In so doing, the definition of 'good' teaching became more contested (a reassessment of purpose necessarily reopens the question of whether something is fit for purpose) and the relative priority given to evaluation increased (the use of 'soft' or short-term funding requires a rolling programme of evaluation and reporting in order to justify further funding).

This trend was reflected in numerous policy initiatives in a variety of sectors, public and private. These developments should not be characterized in straightforwardly positive or negative terms – decisions were, for the most part, taken with reasonable objectives in mind and in good faith – and, without these events, the model of high quality, lifelong, life-wide learning which *may* lie in our future would perhaps not be a possibility at all. The rather volatile reaction that has sparked interest in adult learning presently generates both threats and opportunities for the recognition of effective teaching and effective teachers. In rising to meet these challenges, we shape the future.

Another factor which has contributed heavily to the narrowing conception of teaching and learning has been the apparently general loss of faith in professional groups since the late 1980s. This applies particularly in the context of their ability to act ethically, and to have relevant and worthwhile knowledge of core areas of their professional expertise (Schön 1991). Such a loss of faith in any community leads to the conclusion that the regulation of practice and 'quality control' must be managed by external agents who are assumed to be objective, impartial and transparent in their judgements. In public, private and voluntary sectors, it is generally the case that the recognition of effective teaching has become neither a matter for learners nor teachers, but an outcome of inspection, including direct observation by 'outsiders', and bureaucratic measures of efficiency and 'outputs'.

Although I endorse the need for the evaluation of teaching, especially in the light of the professional's interest in their own competence and society's interest in the effective use of public money, I believe that the criteria by which that evaluation is carried out have become confused. The difficulty in quantifying teaching output has led to a trend to recognize and affirm those limited parts of teaching practice which can be institutionally measured, and the marginalization of those parts which cannot. Compatibility with audit processes has come to define notions of teaching quality, rather than the consistent ability to reflect truly excellent teaching defining appropriate models for quality assurance. Even language has changed: commercial analogies are now commonplace in discussing teaching, in a way that once would have been meaningless or laughable. This problem is not confined to any one sector: a striking example over which I recently stumbled relates to charities engaged in overseas development work, capacity building in target communities through 'teach the teacher' programmes. Although this work is clearly of the highest practical importance, the need to provide data suitable for satisfying the accounting processes of the charity's funding partner led to the distortion of the programme's delivery and outcomes. You could consider your own work: how does your teaching fit into your organizational strategy? Do responsibilities owed to your institution (compliance with internal policy, hierarchical relationship with colleagues, etc.) relate to the improvement of your teaching practice or the experience of learners?

This audit-based approach is exceedingly unfortunate, not only because of the damage it does to the personal esteem of many within the profession of teacher but also (and more significantly still) because it risks the atrophy of rich approaches to teaching which are vital to learners but no longer confer an 'evolutionary advantage' on practitioners. The process by which teaching is recognized serves as a rough form of selection for the teachers we will have tomorrow. Practitioners of teaching styles not suited to present forms of recognition may simply 'die off', in professional terms. At the same time, although these narrower conceptions of teaching largely originated outside the educational community, it is beginning to become clear that they have a normalizing effect, both for long-term practitioners and especially new practitioners who have grown up within the present paradigm. Lacking further professional debate in this area, the practice of teaching will have changed to a remarkable degree. Accordingly, understanding these trends is a practical concern, even more than it is a political one.

Selected approaches to the recognition of teaching

Over the following pages, we will explore some selected approaches to the recognition of teaching. At heart, teachers and learners frame their relationship by their own terms. A good relationship in one context may not be the same as a good relationship in another. Conflicts over teaching practices do arise, but the solution rarely lies in reference to a third party. Strategies for the promotion and protection of ethical conduct are, of course, immensely important – but these are best achieved through a strengthening of professional character, and not a weakening of it.

Approaches to the recognition of teaching can be loosely categorized as 'internal' and 'external'. As we have already seen, the process is relevant to a relatively wide number of contexts, too many to provide an exhaustive analysis of the different possible methodologies here. Generally speaking, therefore, internal approaches to the recognition of teaching relate to how individual teachers evaluate their own practice; external approaches relate to the way they are judged by others. A 'full' evaluation of teaching practice should really draw on both internal and external analyses, as the example with which this chapter concludes demonstrates. Used in combination, the two perspectives represent the kind of stereoscopic view (mentioned in Chapter 1) which is the best way to consider any fundamental question relevant to teaching. In the context of daily life, however, and in teachers' relation to society, managers, politicians and accountants, we must probably be resigned to reliance on one alone, and do our best to advocate in reasonable terms measures for its development and reform. There is an irony that our practice as teachers in a pluralistic and equal society is now informed by constructivist and other modern critical theories; yet we are often judged by that same society on the basis of earlier, absolute, right or wrong models.

External approaches

Institutions, which generally mediate between the top (i.e. national policy-making) levels of those with an interest in the evaluation of teaching and the practitioner's level, adopt a range of ways to encourage and demonstrate that they encourage teachers to aspire to excellence, and that teachers duly do so. Positive approaches ('carrots') include:

- High quality, academically accredited, initial and continuing professional development, made available to suit other priorities under congenial conditions
- Opportunities for promotion on the basis of performance as a teacher
- National and local schemes to recognize 'star' performers
- Incentives to undertake innovation in teaching (e.g. small-scale project grants, opportunities to disseminate and build a reputation at conferences)
- Peer observation of teaching conducted with a light touch to enhance development
- Mentoring to enhance performance and aid progression from novice to expert
- Time to reflect on practice in a creative and purposeful way alone and/or in the company of peers
- Investment in sophisticated mechanisms for research into student perceptions of the teaching process
- Enhanced access to new technologies when applied to teaching ('new toys').

Implicit in this model is the understanding that teachers are extrinsically motivated, welcoming and competing for, such rewards. It is assumed that, even so, this positive reinforcement of desired behaviour is insufficient to guarantee sustained endeavour by all. The 'carrots' are complemented, therefore, by the 'sticks':

- Compulsory training at threshold standard only, tailored to meet narrowly defined competence requirements which may not be 'portable'
- Audits
- Observation of teaching conducted to judge performance against an externally defined standard
- Imposition of sanctions for 'poor' performance
- Heavy workloads
- Records of teaching which are checked and assessed by managers.

Do any of these methods, carrots or sticks, strike a chord with your own practice?

If we compare the lists of carrots and sticks, it becomes apparent that the activities underlying both are, in fact, very similar. The distinction between the two is chiefly in the manner of presentation. It is worth asking, therefore, why the distinction is necessary. If teachers are encouraged to take part in something, clearly understanding how it will work, and standing to gain from the experience, they are likely to be motivated positively, feel confident enough to take manageable risks leading to innovation and to perform at their best. If, however, something appears arbitrary, designed to catch people out, and likely to lead to some form of punishment in the event of failure (as judged by an unknown third party), teachers may be more likely to perform at less than their best and, wherever possible, avoid taking part in the activity at all. Such a reaction in turn leads to further quasi-punitive measures, escalating the situation. In situations where the trigger mechanism for positive or negative recognition approaches appears to be arbitrary, teaching staff are led to participate in the safest possible way. A culture of mere compliance, avoiding the threat and fear of sanctions, may ensure basic competence; it does not, however, provide a sound basis from which to foster excellence.

The framework within which the recognition of teaching is approached is thus immensely significant (although, as we shall see later, not conclusive) in determining the degree to which teachers will respond positively. Quite apart from the real practical difficulties in agreeing how teaching should be recognized and evaluated, the heavy-handedness with which the task is sometimes approached clouds the whole issue in an additional veil of high emotion and obscurity.

Affiliation to professional bodies and commitment to professional updating

The following example is based on experience in the UK, comparable initiatives have also taken place elsewhere or may be about to occur. The National Committee of Inquiry into Higher Education (1997, commonly known as the Dearing Report) proposed, in Recommendation 48, that:

> It should become the normal requirement that all new full-time academic staff with teaching responsibilities are required to achieve at least associate membership of the Institute for Learning and Teaching in Higher Education, for the successful completion of probation.

This was important in two ways. First, it formalized an emerging weight of opinion that novice teachers in higher education might be expected to meet an agreed professional standard. Second, it stopped short of imposing an obligation for formal training, directly controlled by central government (like that required for school teachers). The Institute for Learning and Teaching in Higher Education (ILTHE) was conceived as a membership organization managed by HE professionals on behalf of their peers. There were various ways institutions and individuals could arrange to meet the standard for associate membership of the ILTHE. These routes built on a considerable amount of experience in the sector which had developed over the previous decade. Much of it had been prompted and supported by the Staff and Educational Development Association (SEDA) which had initiated work on an accreditation scheme for teachers in higher education as early as 1990. Recommendation 48 also paved the way for considerable investment in the design and accreditation of formal programmes not only intended to meet particular institutional requirements but also recognized by the ILTHE. Such programmes are now well established and are usually postgraduate certificates (or modules towards them), requiring in the region of 300–600 hours of total learning time at master's level. They are quite diverse in their pedagogy and vary in the emphasis placed on thinking about the practice of teaching within higher education and developing technical competence in doing it. Significantly, even since the ILTHE was replaced by the Higher Education Academy (HEA) in 2003, there has been no pressure to standardize these programmes in a prescriptive 'one size fits all' way.

The approach has been rather different for teachers in the tertiary sector in the UK. Rather than overt organization of a formal professional body, a quasi-regulatory model has been used: there has been a policy shift towards a requirement for teachers to be trained and qualified in a centrally managed system. From June 2008, new teachers in community learning and development, further education, offender learning and work-based learning must be qualified. Additionally, a professional status is expected for all with a mandatory requirement to record at least a minimum quota of continuing professional development. These government requirements are being implemented by the sector skills council, Lifelong Learning (LLUK).

One method to recognize teachers, therefore, is to organize them into more or less formal professional bodies, and to make membership of those bodies contingent upon some sort of commitment to professional development, both initial and continuing. This nod towards the professionalization of teachers in the context of HE should assist in identifying basically competent individuals, and through the use of different levels of affiliation (associate, fellow, senior fellow, for example) assist in discriminating between them. This approach does not evaluate their teaching practice *per se*, but instead permits inferences about their practice from their commitment to their own professional development and/or their ability to meet components of a professional standards framework on the basis of a peer-reviewed application. This approach to recognition effectively sidesteps some of the difficulties we have noted in analysing teaching practice on a large scale; it does not, however, provide any evidence of learning 'throughput' for policy-makers and other interested parties, or record or identify examples of practice (as opposed to practitioners) which should be praised and/or emulated.

The conception of professional body around which this model is built is also more limited than perhaps it could or should be. The professional bodies of teachers do not appear to have the influential public voice enjoyed by longer-standing equivalents from other professions, such as the British Medical Association, the Law Society or the Bar Council. The development of effective teaching, effective teachers and education in general would be enhanced by the capacity for expert practitioners to make consistent contributions to public policy-making. As an example, we might cite the Higher Education Funding Council for England (HEFCE) proposal in 2007 to withdraw funding for adult learners who wish to pursue academic study which leads to equivalent or lower qualifications (ELQS) than those they already hold, even in a different field. Despite a considerable degree of opposition (including criticism from a parliamentary select committee), there has been no success in altering a strategy which many professional groups identify as ill considered, discriminatory and detrimental to national, sectoral and individual interests.

Indeed, in the context of the teaching of adult learners taken as a whole, the rather piecemeal developments in this form of recognition are distinctly ambiguous. They may indicate an acceptance that teaching is a complex, demanding and socially significant activity (like medicine or the practice of law); that is, a *raising* of the professional status of teacher. Alternatively, they may indicate a *loss* of confidence in the quality of practice, requiring remedial action, regulation and external control.

'Consumer' surveys

Surveys of learners and their experiences offer a key way to evaluate the quality of teaching, convenient both for the needs of policy-makers, institutional analysts and, to a certain extent, teaching practitioners. Use of surveys is wide, ranging from the national scale (such as the National Student Survey (NSS) of HE students in England, Wales and Northern Ireland) to the evaluation of a particular course or module conducted by a particular teacher at a particular institution. As such, depending on the way in which the survey is framed, they can provide, in principle, information on large-scale trends (numbers of participants in a sector, the nature of the general experience, employability, etc.) or individual attributes (on such and such a course, a certain percentage of learners preferred topic A to topic B, or found lectures more helpful than seminars, and so on).

There are four key criteria for effective surveys. Questionnaires, usually administered in person, by post or (increasingly) online, must be, first, *reliable*, and second, *valid*. These concepts are familiar in the context of assessment (see also Chapter 4): put simply, an instrument is reliable if it performs consistently. This includes the way that the various parts of the questionnaire may contribute to the whole, and the questionnaire's stability if it is repeated with the same set of subjects. Validity means that the survey actually measures what it claims to measure. Third, for surveys to be *meaningful*, care must be taken in selecting the size of the sample used (ideally, the whole population or, at the very least, a representative part): we must be able to assume that the responses given are typical of the entire community being researched. For example, the NSS assumes that responses from HE students who study the same subjects can reasonably be compared with one another. Fourth, individual questions within the survey must be written in such a way that they do not imply a 'correct' answer and are *free from bias*.

Large-scale surveys are very costly to run but, when done well and repeated over a number of years, they may yield excellent information about trends and how such trends change over time. The results of such surveys tell us, for example, what undergraduate students think about their experience of higher education. The NSS, for example, has surveyed final-year undergraduate students annually since 2005. More detail is available about it on the Higher Education Academy website (www. heacademy.ac.uk). It is a significant component of the Higher Education Funding Councils' revised quality assurance framework (QAF). The very relevance of such surveys to policy-makers also contains the seeds of a potential disadvantage: doing well in the NSS is now of the highest importance for universities, and this has led to the survey reflexively influencing the work being researched. Of itself, the idea that evaluation informs practice is commendable. However, where evaluation is conducted on such a large scale, distinctions in particular circumstance tend to be smoothed out. Measures to improve an institutional NSS score may mean that teaching structures are changed to duplicate those which seem to generate good responses to the survey: even if the institution's student population is in fact distinctive. The NSS gives feedback on the population as a whole and may not take account of distinctive regional or institutional contexts, let alone those of particular groups or individuals. As a result, large-scale surveys to recognize teaching excellence, considered alone, may be somewhat misleading.

Small-scale surveys, of particular groups, are less unwieldy than the NSS or its equivalents. Although all surveys risk failing to identify the particular circumstances of distinct groups, small-scale versions offer a realistic chance for the surveyors to review all the responses, and appropriately reflect them in their conclusions. The peril of small-scale surveys, however, is that they are often badly administered or designed.

The widespread use of 'happy sheets' – brief (one or two A4 sides) surveys which ask very limited questions, usually confined to tick boxes or numerical scales: 'How happy were you with the teaching of this course? Circle a number on the scale from 1–10' – is not well suited to substantial evaluation of teaching practice. As instruments, they have a limited value in identifying whether a particular problem was experienced (as a general rule, happy-sheet scores tend to find a natural average; if a set of scores is very low, a problem may be indicated) but they are often not sufficiently discerning to identify its source reliably. The combination of loosely drafted questions and restricted opportunities for answers can also mean that various extraneous factors affect results. For these reasons, use of happy sheets alone is not a good form of evaluation, although there can be benefits in using them for immediate feedback, with a more considered opportunity for comment made available to learners later on. Teachers might consider alternative methods for obtaining immediate feedback, such as the use of self-adhesive notes to capture participants' immediate impressions (described earlier). Whatever method used, it is always desirable to give learners some opportunity to write open-ended responses, rather than relying solely on closed questions.

Medium to long surveys conducted on a small scale, professionally designed and administered, can be one of the most powerful tools for exploring the performance of a particular teacher or course (see below). However, in most circumstances, measures of this nature are prohibitively expensive, either in terms of formal resources, expertise or cost. In the course of a long teaching career, or a long-established course, evaluations of this type should still be considered on occasion, analogous to a periodic medical check-up. Other, more cost-effective forms of evaluation of this nature might use teachers to design and administer surveys via dedicated software or within the context of a VLE. Teachers who find themselves designing material of this nature should bear in mind the four criteria introduced earlier, as well as the need to be thorough and even-handed, and to give room for the voices of the learners. Follow-up interviews may be appropriate, in some circumstances.

It is worth examining what we are doing when we ask learners to make comments on their learning, and the teaching which has supported it. It is very hard to deny the commonsense proposal that learners are in a unique position to comment upon the performance of their teachers.

You may remember my description of Quentin in Chapter 1. We all tend to remember teachers whom we particularly liked, as well as those who in some way seemed not to have our feelings or interests at heart. There are many circumstances in which learners wish to express publicly their feelings about teachers; one of the real joys of the profession, from schools to colleges to universities to training and development, is the surprising (and sometimes touching) range of responses that we receive from learners. This tendency can be weighed against media horror stories of vicious personal attacks levelled against teachers on websites such as www.ratemyprofessors.com, an American website that has now also gained a foothold in the UK. How should we interpret this variety of behaviour? What, if anything, does it tell us about the teachers and learners concerned? Most importantly, what light does this cast upon the use of learner responses as evidence of effective teaching, acquired either by formal or less formal means?

Proper use of learner responses requires a clear understanding of the role that they are expected to play. To be precise, we need to be sure that we know the function of the learner's opinion within a spectrum of evidence about the quality of teaching. Many problems arise because we (or third-party evaluators) treat comments from participants in learning activities as if they shared our professional understanding of what they were being asked to do, how their comments would be used and agreed to adopt the highest standards of professional practice in expressing their conclusions. Clearly, this is not what always happens. There are two solutions to this problem. Learner feedback can be acknowledged as a very mixed assortment of 'raw' data, and subjected to the highest standards of analysis and interpretation (appropriate to any relevant research paradigm, especially in the social sciences and humanities). The resulting analysis can then be used, with caution, to contribute to an evaluation of teaching provision. Alternatively, teachers can attempt to develop learners into more 'expert' consumers (even 'connoisseurs'; see below) of teaching practice, and thus better able to recognize effective performance on an objective basis. If successful, this method might enable greater weight to be placed on their feedback, especially where the subject matter of their education (as with my students) is the teaching process itself. There is a significant risk to this latter approach, however: it is possible that the coaching required to enable the students to understand the teaching process fully could be misinterpreted as coaching to give the 'right' answers on the survey. An example of this precise situation arose in the British media in 2008, when it was reported that academics in certain universities were placing inappropriate pressure on students to give positive responses to the NSS. Without intimately knowing the particular situation, there is no way of knowing whether those concerned were behaving unethically. It is at least possible, however, that they were aware that most students do not appreciate the responsibility that filling in such surveys involves, and were merely seeking to forestall naïve, facetious or ill-informed answers.

The basis for any analysis of learner responses can be summarized in a few brief questions.

First, have the learners concerned had sufficient relevant experience of the relevant teacher(s) to make a reliable judgement? In practical terms, this question explores whether the survey should require a threshold level of engagement in the course before a learner is eligible to be considered in the survey. Many teachers have commented on the way that institutional systems tend to fail to discriminate between the opinions of learners who have taken part in all or most of the course activities, and those of learners whose attendance or participation have been poor or erratic.

Second, do the learners require technical knowledge of the subject being taught (and the pedagogy being used) in order to make a proper judgement on the quality of their experience? For example, a common concern for teachers of FE and undergraduate HE students revolves around student criticism of learning materials. There may be confusion when the learner believes themselves to be entitled to written material (or even an audio or video recording) covering the content of a face-to-face teaching session in full. The teacher, however, may have designed the material as a supplement to the teaching session, not a substitute for attendance. If that learner's attendance has been poor, and they then seek to rely solely on the written material provided in preparing for assessment, they often conclude that the material is partial and inadequate, rather than recognizing the fact that the deficit is the result of a deliberate pedagogic approach. There is then a tendency to give the teacher a poor evaluation for the course as a whole.

Third, are the learners sufficiently acquainted with their own preferences, so that they can allow for them when making judgements and so avoid personal bias? In other words, can learners recognize teaching that is effective, even if they do not enjoy it or find that it does not suit their personal learning preference? This issue may be characterized in technical terms as the risk of confusing or misunderstanding the teacher's particular 'pedagogic identity' in a given teaching context (Zukas and Malcolm 2002), a 'mask' which may be suitable for particular performances of the teacher's role. One of the teacher's core skills might be considered the ability to adopt the appropriate pedagogic identity in diverse environments. This may be a manifestation of her/his command of the situation, flexibility and professional competence. Alternatively it may be a source of potential difficulty if learners are expecting one mask and are then presented with another. They may have a sense of what 'proper' teachers do and, where there is a mismatch, the learners may express negativity towards the teacher. The mismatch (as perceived by the learners) may be because of the teacher's pedagogic preference in a particular situation or it may arise from institutional or other contextual pressure to behave in a particular way.

Reading learners' feedback (on my own and other people's teaching), I see relatively little evidence of positive answers to these questions. Caution must always be exercised, therefore, in the use to which material of this nature is put. That said, this does remain a vital form of feedback: learners' opinions have a certain intrinsic importance, quite apart from their instrumental value. As teachers, we should take more care in developing learners' ability to recognize positive teaching experiences. This is particularly important when teaching adults who may have had limited experience of being taught as an adult, perhaps none since they were at school or professional training which privileges a particular pedagogic stance. Some of the literature implies that adults will automatically prefer the kind of participative, democratic classroom experience that many teachers of adults value very highly. In fact, this might seem quite disorienting and even threatening to some. Care should be taken when introducing learners to ways of teaching with which they may be unfamiliar. A little time spent on such an introduction and orientation can reduce anxiety, develop understanding and may improve performance. It will reinforce their learning, also making it more likely that they will be better able to recognize excellence in our profession. Of course, to be able to make such introductions requires teachers to have sufficient time in any course or event and an excellent understanding of their own reasons for pedagogic choices. Gaining such understanding and being able to explain it is also likely to improve teaching performance through increased confidence.

Teaching awards

It is worth taking a brief look not only at the external recognition of teaching excellence but also at the way in which it might be celebrated. Skelton (2005) provides a good overview and critical reflection on research undertaken to increase the understanding of teaching excellence as currently conceived in HE. His analysis draws on examples from Australia, Canada, South Africa and the United States to give an international perspective. While the primary focus is clearly HE, the issues and ideas discussed are relevant to practice with adults in any sector. It is worth reading, as the practice of making such awards (which also had early adopters in FE) is becoming more widespread.

Some schemes, such as the HEA's National Teaching Fellowship Scheme, seek to enhance the standing and status of teaching by identifying and rewarding 'outstanding' individual teachers. Others take steps to articulate the social nature of teaching (for example, The Times Higher Awards recognize individuals and groups who innovate and sustain excellence in HE). Whether designed for groups or individuals, all of these models are competitive. They claim to be able to identify winners from the submissions of evidence in support of personal claims. The kinds of evidence, and the nature of the claim it supports, vary. Various learning institutions operate local schemes, in place of (or sometimes in addition to) the national one. In this way, the process can be tailored to reflect their particular strengths, and their aspirations for their staff.

In their ambition to identify and promote positive examples of teaching practice, these initiatives are admirable. However, in having the opportunity to review submissions for awards of this type, several other thoughts struck me.

Taken as a whole, the applications represented an enormous wealth of distinguished work. Choosing between them was almost an arbitrary matter; each application placed emphasis on a different but equally important aspect of the teaching experience. I ended up feeling quite uncomfortable about the process: almost all of the applicants merited recognition of their excellence, and highlighting one instance above another was sometimes a reflection of the personal priorities of the assessors, not an objective judgement on the quality of the teaching.

The model by which evidence is presented in support of applications for this sort of extraordinary recognition of teaching merit may not be sufficiently broad, and thus not sufficiently rigorous. Applications relied chiefly upon self-reporting, a limited amount of peer review and student feedback. Given the symbolic function of teaching awards, I believe that they should reflect an excellent, rather than merely adequate, model for the evaluation of teaching: this necessitates a more subtle appreciation that the way such evidence can be gathered and presented itself represents many disciplinary differences which are beyond the control of individual teachers. Teachers in some disciplines routinely work with large numbers of undergraduates who are required to generate relatively large volumes of responses to teaching which are analysed centrally. This provides apparently 'hard' evidence of performance with little or no effort by the individual teacher. Other disciplines' teaching practices make it much more difficult for individual teachers to generate any evidence which can be presented in support of their case for excellence.

On the basis of these observations, I am not convinced that the case for teaching awards has been clearly made. They represent a step to address the negative institutional climate which, unfortunately, sometimes tends to contaminate the evaluation of teachers – but not one that is sufficiently conceptualized. A preferable approach might be the harder one, which would acknowledge the complexity of recognizing good teaching and the importance of a broad approach to gathering and presenting appropriate evidence in support of claims to excellence. Such claims might also recognize the collective responsibility for most teaching success. It is very rare indeed for an excellent teacher to be sure that they alone deserve the glory.

Internal approaches

In exploring and evaluating their own teaching, teachers often resort to the following approaches. In many ways, these approaches can, do and should inform the types of evaluative exercise that we have considered in the previous pages.

Reflective practice as a qualitative evaluation method

While there is significant difference between approaches taken to the initial development of teachers in adult learning, perhaps the most dominant discourse concerns reflective practice.

It is assumed that initial training or professional affiliation inducts professionals into a sustained (and largely unquestioned) culture of continuing professional development which facilitates progress from novice to expert. As yet, neither the precise form of initial nor continuing development is defined prescriptively for much of the field. It is expected that individuals will assume responsibility for adherence to an ethical code, keeping themselves up to date, adjusting to systemic change in working conditions and be competent in the use of new technologies. There may also be a tacit assumption that they will also become skilful managers of curricula, student administration, budgets and facilities. A reflective practice model can be a powerful tool in evaluating one's performance as a teacher (as well, in some cases, as the performance of others), and can lead to action-oriented outcomes which are appropriate for CPD.

The concept of reflective practice relates, at least in part, to the ethnographic research method, developed in the social sciences (and especially anthropology). It comprises various techniques, most commonly including participant observation, interviews, critical incident analysis, keeping personal journals and discourse analysis. These techniques are focused on investigating how a specific group actually works. They accept that any description and analysis will be influenced by the person of the researcher; rather than trying to eliminate it, therefore, strenuous efforts are made to represent the influence as honestly as possible and to work with it. Ethnographic methods are particularly helpful in providing rich pictures of specific situations, enabling the researcher to appreciate what was going on at a particular place at a particular time. Recognizing their own limitations, ethnographic researchers may often consult members of the group being studied to see if they recognize themselves in the description and explanations being put forward. Conclusions are generally tentative, and any recommendations which may emerge are generally framed narrowly to the people who took part in the study, or those who can be reliably identified as being very much like them.

Generally more economical in the use of resources, as well as naturally suited to the nature of the task, ethnographic methods are currently used for significant amounts of research into learning and teaching. Small in scale, the data are often qualitative and need local interpretation rather than statistical treatment. It may not be replicable and, as such, policy-makers tend to be suspicious of its use. Some of the research which uses ethnographic methods is characterized as 'action-research' (Winter 1989). This method is employed when teachers are encouraged to inquire in a systematic and purposeful way into their own teaching. The intention is not to generate outcomes which must be adopted by others. Rather, it is to illuminate what is currently taking place in a particular situation in order to improve upon it. This kind of systematic process (activity, collection of evidence about what actually happened, interpretation of the evidence to suggest options for development leading to adjustments in performance) contributes substantially to the approach often described as reflective practice. It is important for several reasons.

First, reflective practice enables teachers to sustain interest in their own teaching. I am unlikely to be an effective teacher if I lose interest in what is happening with learners and the material being learned. Not only does reflective practice point towards action for personal or professional development, but also it provides motivation for it.

Second, reflective practice can lead to improvement in any or all aspects of teaching practice. It emphasizes a rolling process of self-evaluation, which makes the teacher more likely to attend fully to their learners (see Chapter 6) and leads into a process of experimentation and development of personal practice which is conducive to innovation and expert performance.

Third, and of particular relevance to this chapter, evidence that a teacher practises reflectively may itself be a meaningful indication of effective teaching. It is rarely sufficient on its own, but when placed alongside student feedback, student achievement and peer observation, it can have considerable importance. The truth of this is indicated by the tendency in courses for the initial formation of teachers of adults to base summative assessment on, among other aspects, evidence of reflection on practice.

For all these reasons, reflective practice is an important component in the evaluation of teaching and one that, in its particular approach, fills a gap in the various external approaches to the recognition of teachers and teaching. Readers are strongly encouraged to explore this model in further detail, not only to equip them more fully for their work but also to accredit them as ambassadors for a process which has the potential to make a great difference to this area of professional practice.

Connoisseurship

Complementary to the idea of reflective practice, which is chiefly concerned with teachers examining themselves, is the idea of connoisseurship, which can offer a model for people in the know (other teachers, and conceivably learners) to examine the teacher.

Any performance is open to critique. We may reflect on how well something has been done privately (which often comes down to how much we enjoyed it), or we may deploy a set of previously agreed criteria in a detached and personally disinterested way. In the case of the arts, sport and other aspects of the leisure industry (restaurants, hotels and amenities) critics may be employed to make such judgements for us. Even though they also vary in their position along the subjective–objective continuum, reputations are made (and lost) as a result of such expert views. We might assume that they were selected for their own professional expertise in recognizing excellence. We might refer to them as 'connoisseurs'. Pye (2007: 18, citing Prown 1993) proposes that 'connoisseurship is based on extensive knowledge and is a "powerful scholarly tool, permitting rapid distinction between what is true and what is false".'

Given the difficulties that we have identified with learner feedback, and the role that the judgements of our peers make in other instances of institutional recognition of teaching practice, the case has already been implicitly made for a model of connoisseurship in teaching. However, in giving it a name and an identity, its value should be even easier to articulate. Professional analogies abound. For example, it is true to say that proof of the success of a restaurant is defined by its ability to stay in business and to make a profit. This requires that it satisfies its customers, maintains a sustainable client base, responds to feedback, and so on. However, it is also true to say that proof of the success of a restaurant depends upon the constructive comment of professional critics, nourishing the professional flair of the kitchen staff, prompting innovation and development, and attracting new and wider audiences for the chef's virtuosity. Both of these analyses are correct, but neither tells the whole story by itself. The true measure of success is the combination of the two, even though in strict terms their relationship may be hard to analyse. Teaching is no different.

Putting oneself to the test: one experience of evaluation

Aside from the official, mostly large-scale techniques used for the evaluation of teaching, I was interested to experiment with the process myself. To do this, I invited an academic colleague to conduct a study of my own teaching performance. This would enable me to review my own practice (both individually and in dialogue with others) for the purposes of professional development, to consider questions of curricular design related to my teaching responsibilities, and to investigate whether a 'Rolls Royce' model of evaluation is useful and practicable. I was also interested to explore how it felt to have my professional practice subjected to such scrutiny. A fuller account of this project will be published in the future but, for the present, it can be summarized in the following terms.

All those who had taken part in a particular group of taught modules (representing my principal teaching commitments) in the period 2002–2008 were invited to take part in the study. They were given a short questionnaire, delivered electronically, and then invited for interview in person or by telephone at a convenient date in the following weeks. All responses were anonymized, and the interviews were conducted by an individual who had no prior contact with the courses from which the modules were drawn, or the participants who were surveyed. On completing the information gathering phase, the researcher completed a lengthy report of the findings (15–20 pages), which was compiled, structured and drafted following some consultation on appropriate questions, lines of enquiry and preliminary readings of the questionnaire results with me. For the purposes of the present discussion, that report is treated as the outcome to the study. For other professional purposes, the researcher is now in the process of editing the document to produce an accurate, permanent record in consultation with a teacher colleague and me.

(Professional journal entry)

I was very happy with the professionalism of my colleague, and the way in which the study was executed. From it, I took the following insights, some anticipated, and some not.

The most striking thing about the experience was my emotional response to it. In the course of 35 years' teaching, I have become used to having my work reviewed by others, operating in a range of contexts, and I am prone to reflecting extensively on my own practice. I have long known how much my sense of personal worth is wrapped up with the recognition of my professional competence, and I have developed strategies to protect and sustain myself when this process makes life uncomfortable. Nonetheless, even though I was the initiator of the whole endeavour, I found the process surprisingly stressful. The feeling of being judged, of banked-up fear, indignation, and even resentment, was acute. When reading the final report, passages praising my performance initially passed me by, while passages which I judged to be overly harsh caused me considerable pain.

Does this mean the exercise was too costly personally? Of course not. Rereading the report with a critical friend, he understood it in quite a different way than I had. Indeed, viewed by a third party, the report was very positive: my response seems to have been acute not because the accounts were negative but largely because the voice recalling them was not my own, and therefore differed from my interpretation in innumerable small ways. Despite my own position of power in the particular evaluation process (its initiator, designer, arbiter of its validity and so on), I reacted as if I had no personal agency and was entirely vulnerable. Thus, the first, and most important, conclusion I can tentatively draw from the experience is that, no matter how positively an evaluation of this kind is framed, it may not always feel good for its subject! It is important for teachers, and any professional undergoing a similar experience, to be prepared for this feeling, and to find strategies to cope with it. When critiquing the means by which our professional talent is recognized, it is obviously of particular importance to distinguish consciously between arguments which develop out of a sense of vulnerability and even exploitation (which may not be always trustworthy); and 'hard', neutral arguments relating to deficiencies in method.

From the breakdown of the report, it was clear that the follow-up interviews conducted with the participants went a long way towards clarifying and extending their responses in the questionnaires. The researcher's experience certainly demonstrated the trend, already noted earlier, in the occasional fallibility of learners' perceptions. The researcher's opportunity to talk with them seemed to assist considerably in the analytical process which followed, attempting to discount irrelevant information reliably while fully and accurately presenting the meaning of their core contributions. Even so, and certainly through no individual fault, the 'processed' feedback which ultimately featured in the researcher's report reflected a certain distance from my own, professional understanding of the reality. The feedback it contained was tailored to a conception of the curriculum and my personal teaching style, but it did not in all particulars match my own understanding of what I was doing. In itself, this insight is obviously of relevance to my own professional development. No matter how experienced a teacher you are, there is always the potential for a certain amount of your substance or approach to be 'lost in translation'. At the same time, it underlines that a connoisseur's evaluation is a vital complement, even to one of the most thorough pieces of teaching evaluation I have seen in my professional career. The critical friend, who read the report with me, was able to nuance the substance of the report in the light of his own, expert opinion of my teaching performance, drawing out key areas for my direct attention and offering alternative interpretations of others. Not only was his input helpful in making sense of the feedback I was offered, but also the nature of our dialogue was immensely helpful and constructive. Walking through a process of this kind in company, our sense of shared professional character was enhanced, our practice honed, and our ability to engage with the realities of our strengths and weaknesses developed.

One final point should be mentioned. The evaluation undertaken was of immense professional and developmental interest. Nonetheless, it is *extremely* unlikely that it will advance the recognition of my skill and status outside the classroom to any extent, or that of the profession as a whole. The process is too subjective, and the outcome too nuanced, for it to set the world on fire. It is important for teachers, as a group, to consider the way in which they are recognized, and to lobby for a more effective approach, if only to promote and protect a realistic conception of teaching and learning in public policy. In so doing, we must walk a difficult path between honesty about the relative significance of various approaches and expediency. Deep evaluation of our practice, however, is likely to remain only of intrinsic value, a manifestation of our personal commitment to learning and growth. It can help to make us great teachers, but perhaps not celebrated ones.

The model of evaluation described in this section is obviously not practical as a matter of routine. The cost of the researcher's time alone would be prohibitive on a day-to-day basis. The underlying principles, however, are relevant to the approaches to recognition we have discussed; and the experience of conducting the survey confirms that 'deep' evaluation exercises of this kind may be of great professional value when circumstances will permit them to be carried out. I am very glad to have done it.

Several practical comments are worth noting here:

- Teachers should volunteer for such evaluation when they are ready to do so: a degree of confidence in practice is a helpful balance to the feelings otherwise inspired by such close dissection.

- The project should ideally be managed by a team of three: subject, researcher and critical friend.
- All results must be anonymized.
- The process of anonymization is complex and can distort the results or reduce their usefulness.
- Management of the scope and scale of the study is important and not easy: the idea of the approach is that the evaluation is as deep as possible, yet it is easy to design an approach that is unfeasible or unrealistic.
- Results should be reported privately to the subject and the critical friend.
- Key themes should be agreed between the three members of the project team.
- The key themes should be made public.
- Outcomes should be shared with the learners who took part in the project.
- Dialogue should be encouraged with colleagues, learners and other interested parties in the light of the evaluation outcomes, and with a view to developing practice.

Conclusion

We can characterize many of the issues concerned with the recognition of teaching by reference to other perspectives, borrowing from much wider social and historical patterns. In the history of art, the changing status of the artist is viewed as a valid subject for investigation. Such change has impacted on the production, interpretation and value placed upon works of art. I have been struck by the parallels between discussion of the status of 'artist' and my current thinking about teachers. Barker et al. (1999) discuss significant change in status for artists in sixteenth-century Italy which would subsequently resonate across Europe and America. The drivers for change in status for renaissance artists which might have some correspondence with change in status as a teacher in contemporary England include:

- Adoption of emerging technologies
- New ways of organizing training and work (from craft guilds to an academy)
- Varied relationships with allied trades
- Different sources of funding and 'patronage'
- Celebration of individual talent occasionally reinforced by a mythology of 'genius'

- Accumulation of evidence to assert relative importance as a practitioner including 'self-portraits', biographical writing and *oeuvre* (a collection of work or outcomes of practice), that is, a kind of portfolio of evidence in support of a claim for recognition.

Put simply, there was a shift from collective, craft-based, conservative, individually commissioned working practices towards individually attributed work inspired by personal creativity which embraced new technologies and was often dependent upon funding from the state and/or other large organizations (e.g. the Roman Catholic Church or commerce). Similar changes seem to have occurred during my 35 years of professional involvement with teaching. They have made the practicalities of recognizing effective teaching at an individual level far from straightforward. This is because:

- Judgements of teaching quality are made from diverse perspectives;
- The nature of appropriate evidence may not be agreed;
- Appropriate evidence (even if agreed) may not be available;
- Variables are difficult to isolate, making causal connections controversial.

The discussion in this chapter has illustrated these points. We have looked at the use of large-scale data collection models (such as the NSS), generating a generic conception of what most good teachers of adults are likely to have in common, irrespective of context. We have considered the strengths and weaknesses of this approach, and compared them to insights made from more local perspectives. We have also considered the role played by inferences of professionalism, sometimes made by professional peers, grounded in membership of relevant professional groupings and commitment to professional development.

For the purposes of the 'external' world, professional teachers need to develop their own robust sense of professional character through a combination of evidence-based externally validated measures, reflective practice and a well-articulated sense of values. This may grow, at least in part, from a clear sense of our own 'internal' practice in recognizing and acknowledging excellent teaching. A model for the evaluation of teaching based on thoughtful research, reflective practice and connoisseurship offers the most powerful, and most honest, way ahead.

4 Assessment:
Functional analysis and a typology of individual difference

No work on adult teaching is complete without an exploration of assessment. This is not surprising, given the fundamental relationship that exists between teaching and assessment when fully conceived. In discussing assessment, however, there remains a tendency to divorce it from the teaching and learning process, and to attempt to impose definite rules on 'good' and 'bad' practice. This chapter introduces assessment within the context of the teacher's professional responsibilities, and situates it as yet another strand in the learning relationship.

In order to address these issues, we shall first consider the values and purposes of assessment. Afterwards, we shall look at one particular model which comes within the spectrum of essentialist theories of human personality, and seeks to explore how people vary in the way that they absorb information and make judgements about the world. It makes an excellent basis for further thought in this area. Finally, we shall explore some practical implications of this approach, as well as its limitations.

Let us begin with another story.

> Jess was taking a 15-credit, master's level module as an introduction to reflective practice for her own CPD. It was taught as a stand-alone short course, with the option of completing the assessment for credit. Just as the final face-to-face session was finishing, Jess said to me: 'But aren't you going to tell us how well we have done in the module?' 'What a good question!', I replied, grinning. Jess looked puzzled, even irritated by my failure to give a straight answer to an apparently reasonable request. However, a moment later, she smiled, said: 'Ah, I get it . . . good bye!' and left the room. A couple of weeks later, reading her journal, it became clear that she had grasped, in that moment, many of the aspects of the module which had previously eluded her.

Jess's insight, triggered by the requirement to consider her own question, was much more significant than an off-the-cuff assessment from me would have been. In particular, she was prompted to reflect upon her expectations, hopes and even fears of the answer, and thus to explore the purpose of her question. She might have wanted personal affirmation that we had been glad she was a part of the group – a kind of 'psychological stroking' – or reassurance that it was 'allowed' to spend so much time on her own development. Alternatively, she might have been requesting my opinion of her competence in a particular set of professional techniques; a process of 'benchmarking' to confirm fitness to practice. It is even possible she hoped to be told she was the best (or at least not the worst) member of the group, in order to compare her performance with that of her peers. All of these are legitimate functions for assessment – and they are all too important to be improvised, especially at the end of a long day.

Jess realized that she had inadvertently laid a trap, both for me as teacher and for herself as learner: she did not really know what she was asking. As such, no matter what answer I chose to give, my response would probably not have been satisfactory to her – and might easily have been problematic for other participants who overheard our exchange. I could so easily have relied upon one interpretation of the question and been very wide of the mark. Moreover, in accepting the role of 'expert' (implicit in the format of assessment she had sought to impose), I would have undermined the pedagogy of the whole module, which was centred upon the individual's role in reflecting upon and evaluating their own practice.

Fortunately, Jess realized the implications of her original request, and went on to ask some very precise and searching questions about her own practice in her reflective journal. Some of these she expressly addressed to me so that I could respond in a considered and private way in written feedback. The rest she answered for herself. In so doing, she demonstrated that she had understood the difficulties of the original form of assessment she had sought to employ (no clearly defined outcome, potentially inappropriate method) and adopted a better strategy in response. She had taken responsibility for identifying and resolving many of the problematic issues underlying assessment just in the way a good teacher should.

This simple anecdote illustrates three subtleties that underlie this topic.

First, no teacher can say they are not concerned with assessment. Wherever in the spectrum of adult learning your practice is situated, one way or another you *will* be involved in assessing learning. In some situations, it may have a higher profile or be more apparently technical – but it is never entirely absent. Susan Oosthuizen's accessible and aptly named *Probably the Shortest Introduction to Assessing Adult Students in the World* (2002) may be useful, if you are entirely new to the task of assessing adult learning.

Second, even the teacher may not see assessment coming: it is not always teacher initiated, and may not occur in a 'traditional' format (an essay, an exam paper, etc.). As such, even in apparently 'non-assessed' courses, it may be very difficult to avoid some form of judgement of learning. Jess's question, whether it remained unspoken or asked out loud, illustrates that learners need to know how they are getting on with the work of learning. It is the responsibility of teachers to know what and when to tell them, and when to keep silent so that they can learn to trust their own judgement. Jess was ready to be trusted to answer her own question – but how had she reached this point? And, of equal importance for us as teachers, how did I know that she had?

Third, assessment is not a mechanistic task. It is intrinsically related to the substantive content being learned, and can either consummate it or destroy it. In Jess's case, as a student who wished to learn about reflective practice, would an off-the-cuff assessment from another person – even her teacher – be truly compatible with the basic principles she was trying to learn?

For very good reasons, therefore, the approach to assessment is one of the hallmarks of a teacher's practice.

Rather than conceptualizing assessment as a necessary chore, let us look at it as an opportunity to increase the power of learning. As such, we shall concentrate on positive approaches. We shall consider why it often seems to be less than enjoyable for all concerned and explore ways to deal with conflicts of interest which may lie at the heart of problems. In fact, there is no fundamental reason why assessment has to be seen negatively. With a better understanding, we can aim to ensure that assessment provides feedback which nourishes and serves learning, rather than spoiling or detracting from it. In other words, assessment should – and can – be more like plant food than weed killer.

Purposes and values of assessment

Why do we assess learning? As Jess's story illustrated, differences in our answers may result from differences in the way we define assessment itself. This definition from Stephen Brookfield is a good place to start:

> It is particularly important to distinguish evaluation from assessment. These two terms are often used interchangeably, yet they are fundamentally different. The reason for their apparent interchangeability is that the institutional mode of evaluation stresses a value-free checking (assessment) of whether or not certain previously specified objectives have been ascertained. It is apparent that the term assessment, if applied to this latter activity, is being accurately used. Assessment is a value-free

ascertainment of the extent to which objectives determined at the outset of a programme have been attained by participants. Assessment of these objectives requires no value judgement as to their worthwhileness. It is simply a non-judgemental checking as to whether or not certain purposes have been attained.

(Brookfield 1986: 263–4)

I propose four principal purposes for assessment, which also go some way to explaining why it is a vital aspect of learning.

Assessment has the potential to:

- *Provide encouragement*, promote a feeling of safety and build confidence in the learner
- *Orient* the learner within the learning process, providing augmented feedback on progress
- *Benchmark* against a standard
- *Determine appropriate access* to groups, ascribe status within them, confer (or deny) titles, rights, responsibilities, privileges, access to resources, and so on, on the members of groups.

More concisely, we can describe these purposes in technical terms (motivational, formative, summative and certifying); or as part of a journey metaphor: assessment provides 'sustenance' (potentially both emotional and content-related, reinforcing the learning process itself), 'navigation' (through the learning process), 'a postcard home' (communicating where the learner has been and what they have done) and a 'passport' (identifying the learner as part of a particular community).

Teachers need to know how, and when, to help to keep the learning show on the road. Assessing who needs what kind of encouragement, and when they need it most, is not an insignificant aspect of the teacher's role. Even deciding to initiate an assessment of the learner's work – or to respond to a learner's request for assessment – requires a preliminary (and even less formal) assessment by the teacher. In other words, before conducting any *substantive* assessment (which may be directed to any of the four purposes we have identified), a teacher should make an *assessment of need*. This latter process should have a direct consequence on the teacher's identification of relevant assessment purposes, and selection of methodology. It will, ideally, take account of learners' appraisal of their own targets for learning.

Let us briefly unpack these ideas in turn.

It is important to note that one assessment exercise may contribute to a number of these assessment purposes (although some combinations are more common than others), or that each purpose may be addressed separately. The method of assessment selected should be tailored to the needs of the learners and the subject being taught.

As a general rule, the purposes in the earlier list should be considered cumulatively. Preparation and feedback well in advance of any certifying assessment are important to success. Learners need to understand what is required of them and have the opportunity to practise in order to build confidence.

For example, it is perfectly acceptable to provide learners only with motivational assessment (a common practice in the context, for example, of 'leisure learning') or to teach a formal course which meets all four assessment purposes, such as an Advanced level subject, which relies on classroom assessment by the teacher (motivational, formative), mock assessment papers (formative) and final examinations (summative, certifying) or indeed to do anything in between. The only combination which makes for a *bad* teaching experience is an attempt to make assessments for the purposes of benchmarking or certifying without also including opportunity for motivational and formative assessment. Such an approach is counterproductive as it tends to depress learner performance while it also reinforces inappropriate and sometimes painful power relations between learners and teachers. Teaching adults is at best a shared endeavour. Teachers and learners work together towards commonly understood learning outcomes.

Food for thought: assessment as sustenance

Sensitively managed, well-timed opportunities to check progress towards a particular outcome – and the feedback associated with them – can be an important boost to the learner's confidence, self-esteem, motivation, enjoyment and commitment. Such *low stakes* practice (with plenty of opportunity to learn comfortably from one's own mistakes) builds capacity before challenges with more serious consequences must be faced. Whether planned or spontaneous, this kind of assessment recognizes what the learning process costs the learner (whether making time to attend face-to-face classes, take part in online learning, write assignments or simply keep a date with a book) and provides them with sustenance to carry on. It can build confidence, mark the recognition of the learner as an individual as well as part of a group, and spare embarrassment or feelings of childishness. In certain circumstances, it can model the very thing which is being taught, or provide a forum for learners to experiment on their own behalf. The focus of this assessment is thus the *sustenance* of the learner, equipping them to carry on with the learning process through the delivery of motivational feedback.

This book is, of course, about teaching *adults*: it must be asked whether the sustenance model of assessment is superfluous in this context. Much of the literature describes adult learners in very inspiring terms (variously, as autonomous, self-directing, problem-orientated, rich with experience and so on). Thus, at least by implication, a key character-istic of the adult learner is their self-sufficiency. This is a key theme of the 'andragogical' model, popularized by Knowles (1980, 1984, 1990, 1996). In this context, it may seem a little odd to stress the importance of providing sustenance for adults' learning – by assessment or, indeed, by any other means. Nonetheless, as the emphasis in this book on the importance of teachers to adult learners implies, I do not believe that it is so simple.

It is true that adults *can* be as self-sufficient as the andragogical model implies, yet it is not necessarily true that *all* adults manifest that quality *all* the time. We ignore this sophistication at our peril. Not all adult learners are present by choice. Retraining or new requirements in relation to conditions of service may prompt 'conscription' to pro-grammes of study. Certainly, it may not be assumed that learners of any kind – including adults – always possess an ample supply of resources with which to 'pay the bill' for their study. Sooner or later, everyone requires a degree of reinforcement and encouragement.

Moreover, although adults enjoy many advantages as learners, they are also often operating in less than 'optimum' circumstances. Most adults combine learning with work and domestic obligations. Making space to learn – no matter the degree of commitment – remains costly. Even those individuals whose employers or family subsidise and support their learning incur opportunity costs: there are countless moments when learning is intimidating or, at least, subject to competing priorities.

For these reasons, teachers of adult learners need to be chameleons, ready to step in as required by the learner, and adapt themselves to whatever form the learner requires. These teachers need to include both pedagogical and andragogical approaches in their metaphorical 'toolbox' – and it is most certainly true that motivational assessment is a vital aspect of this.

Here is another story. Think how assessment is a factor operating within it, more or less unacknowledged.

Recruited to a British university as a technical expert in her field, Professor George was appointed supervisor for a part-time research master's student, Julian. Now living some distance from the univer-sity, Julian had previously been a successful and highly motivated undergraduate in the department which George joined. Julian maintained full-time working commitments throughout the period in which he was also studying.

About half-way through the supervision period, the relationship between George and Julian unfortunately deteriorated. Professor George imagined her role to be purely academic and editorial: she expected sample chapters to arrive every few months for her to correct. She assumed that Julian's work would develop incrementally, and that Julian's critical sense of his writing would flourish only from this process.

Julian, on the other hand, found it hard to make the necessary time to write up his research to his own satisfaction. He assumed that showing George what he knew to be a substandard piece of work – and receiving feedback on a substandard piece of work – would be of benefit neither to him nor George. He imagined that it was preferable to seek George's input only at the point at which he could not exercise a critical attitude to his work himself.

Sadly, neither George nor Julian managed to achieve a relationship of mutual understanding and compromise. About two-thirds of the way through the supervision period, George appeared to give up on the relationship and declined to accept any responsibility for the outcome of Julian's work.

Julian completed his studies alone, and successfully submitted his work for examination.

The most evident aspect of this story is the importance of the relationship between George and Julian; if the relationship had been different, their difference of opinion might have been resolved more easily. On this point, however, it is important to note that neither was necessarily the 'bad guy': in fact, both supervisor and student needed guidance and support in recognizing and overcoming legitimate challenges. For whatever reason, they were not equipped to do so.

Underlying the story was a difference of opinion about assessment, both about its significance and its function. In the context of a supervised research degree, the most formal – and most obvious – example of assessment is in the submission of the thesis for examination. This final procedure primarily serves two of the purposes of assessment: summative and certifying (the 'postcard home' and the 'passport'). Long before this point, however, the student often receives periodic, less formal assessment by the supervisor through the submission of drafts. This assessment, certain administrative requirements of the university aside, reflect the other two purposes we have identified: motivational and formative. As the story of George and Julian illustrates, there is a very real question whether these forms of assessment are helpful – even achievable at all – if there is not a measure of consensus between teacher and learner about their object and method. We do not really know what purpose George thought Julian's submission of drafts would serve, or even whether George identified the process as one of assessment at all. At least one reading of the situation, however, would suggest that George's failure to account for Julian's motivational needs also ultimately frustrated the (positive) formative purpose that she may have intended.

'Where am I going? Where have I got to?': assessment as navigation

You will probably have recognized this second type of assessment as 'formative assessment'. Its function is to aid progress in learning by the provision of 'orienting' feedback, assisting the learner in navigating themselves to their destination. In the context of a course of learning viewed as a whole, this kind of feedback can be described as the Goldilocks model ('This porridge is too hot . . . too cold . . . just right!') or, more formally, successive approximation or the shaping of behaviour. It may occur informally and spontaneously during working sessions or social contact (as with Jess), or it can be a planned and deliberate activity scheduled for critical points in a particular course or event (as George perhaps envisaged it). Formative assessment and feedback is an integral activity to teaching; a shrewd teacher can contrive to provide at least small amounts to learners in almost any teaching context. Any discussion of this form of assessment thus verges on a discussion of the practice of teaching itself.

It is frequently – although not always – possible to make a single assessment exercise fulfil both motivational and formative functions, our first two purposes for assessment. As the following passage indicates, the two are often intimately related, especially for novice learners. Nonetheless, as the anecdote about Charlie (see pp. 100–1) illustrates, even the decision to pursue multiple purposes in a single assessment should be treated thoughtfully: Charlie's misinterpretation of the context of his tutor's feedback had disturbing consequences for them both.

Different approaches to instructional design focus on alternative ways of breaking learning into tasks and then sequencing them (Cranton 1989). The teacher must consider what sequence is appropriate to the needs of the learner, and the context in which they are operating. The capacity for the tasks to form a basis for meaningful formative assessment is one potentially important criterion. In teaching a process, such as driving a car, it is not necessarily most helpful to begin by teaching the learner to manoeuvre out of a tight parking space. Learners may benefit from the initial experience of achieving success at a relatively basic test (driving a car round an empty car park), not least so they have sufficient confidence to accept and interpret formative feedback on more difficult challenges. Then again, in other contexts, learners may benefit from immersion in (safe versions of) experiences quite beyond their existing competence:

Kevin, one of a minority of young men in a small village, was asked if he would join the local choir, in need of his support. 'But I don't know how,' he said. He knew that the number of men in his voice part (bass) was very small; he was concerned that the inevitable errors he would make in the process of learning would detract from the effect made by the choir as a whole and that such incompetence would make him look stupid.

Fortunately, the choir was scheduled to sing a much larger (and technically somewhat more complicated) work than normal, with the support of a number of borrowed singers from nearby parishes. The choir director firmly encouraged Kevin to come and rehearse for this work only, singing in the midst of a large group of competent basses. To his surprise, he delighted in the experience. Discovering how it felt to sing a large choral piece, before he could actually do it, gave him the confidence to sing with the choir on a regular basis, and, through challenging him to attempt something difficult, gave him a practical basis of experience upon which he could draw in making sense of subsequent practice.

This anecdote highlights one of the conceptual ambiguities about formative assessment. It is important, of course, that the teacher is truthful with the learner (not least to preserve the integrity of their relationship), and gives them (or creates circumstances for them to obtain) accurate feedback on their performance. At the same time, what counts as true feedback may vary somewhat according to circumstance. From his apparently deep-end immersion into the choir, Kevin gained various insights. He was (very!) aware that he was not an experienced singer yet the experience of being surrounded by a large number of competent colleagues gave him an apparently genuine experience of what it would be like to be so, and a certain (if vague) sense of what he needed to do to improve. This kind of feedback was highly appropriate for a beginner – but would not be a good service to an individual preparing for more formal (summative) assessment of their practice.

Teachers draw upon training and experience to attend selectively to the elements most likely to aid progress, and direct the learners' attention accordingly. This process is called augmented feedback, as it adds to or shapes the feedback on progress which learners obtain for themselves. The teacher's experience and perspective may also allow them to guide the learner to what seems a less 'direct' route towards the desired outcome. Sometimes continuing to work on a challenging assignment is a good experience for any adult learner. It can also be the case that being redirected in order to travel a different path towards the same goal ensures that time and energy is not being used up in failure to progress.

Formative assessment need not necessarily be conducted solely by teachers; the use of peers as assessors, in appropriate (and safe) circumstances, can also be a powerful approach. Teachers do retain an important refereeing or quality assurance function, but involvement in making carefully considered comments of the work of one's peers is a useful aid to learning in many situations.

There is, however, one note of caution to be sounded here. It is possible to check too much. It can be a bit like pulling a recently planted bulb out of the ground to see how well the roots are growing. Over-assessment, however well intentioned, will exhaust everyone and imply a lack of confidence in the learners or in yourself as the teacher. Sometimes things just need to run along for a while before you check to see how they are doing. This can be quite scary. It takes experience to build confidence to recognize the time to check and the time to trust.

Talking to the folks back home: assessment as communication

Having read the last pages, you might be quick to point out that all the forms of assessment discussed relate to communication in one form or another. This is true. The third purpose of assessment, which we commonly call summative assessment, is indeed also concerned with communication – but in a fashion which can be interpreted by the wider world, and not necessarily only by the learner in the context of their experience. To apply the journey metaphor, this form of assessment is the flag raised on the mountain top once it has been conquered, or the postcard home on arrival at the holiday destination. It communicates a simple message of achievement: 'how far did the learner get?'.

In technical terms, summative assessment contributes to the formal calculation of the final result (if relevant) of the learning activity. It is the type of assessment which first leaps to most people's minds. Its purpose is to indicate success, in whole or in part, or failure. It is a benchmarking activity. Literally, a 'benchmark' is 'a surveyor's mark cut in some durable material . . . to indicate the starting, closing or any suitable intermediate point in a line of levels for the determination of altitudes over the face of a country' (*Oxford English Dictionary*). Summative assessment shares similar qualities to this definition: it is a durable record of the contours of an individual's learning experience. Regardless of how many (or how few) trouble to look at it, it is presented in a manner which accurately represents a fixed point. This is the obvious category of 'examination'. It is summative in that it takes place either at the conclusion of a course of learning or if the summative assessment is distributed throughout the course (as in modular programmes), it contributes to the final result whenever learners are asked to do it. Its purpose is to indicate success, or degrees of success, or lack of success.

Accreditation is based upon the results of summative assessment and so it is particularly important that it is judged to be fair. This commonsense concept of fairness looks quite innocent but can be slippery. So let us keep it quite simple. First, you may want to think for a few moments about all the kinds of testing and measuring which we use to make judgements on people's ability to do things. Fairness in such situations requires that the instruments used stand a reasonable test of validity. In other words they must measure what they claim to measure. Second, they must be relied upon to do so consistently. This generally means that standards are established against which judgements can be made.

I will briefly describe two ways to do this. They are known as criterion referencing and norm referencing. When an external standard for measuring performance is applied (for example in field athletics the height or length of a jump can be measured and results compared to a preset standard to see which athletes qualify to take part in a particular competition). This is known as criterion referencing. Staying with athletics as an example we could also apply norm referencing. To do this we would measure the distances jumped by all the competitors at an athletics meeting and select the ten longest ones to qualify for the final. The choice of one form of referencing or the other as the means by which to set the standard will tend to generate different outcomes. When teachers and learners are working with known standards, more people tend to achieve them as time passes. This is probably because the teachers improve their ability to guide learning more effectively towards those activities and understandings which are essential to secure success. When learners take an assessment which is norm referenced (in other words they are competing against the other people taking the test rather than trying to achieve a preset standard) the quality of the successful participants may fluctuate. In any given occasion on which the test is offered those that pass may be better or worse than those who passed last time.

Within the scope of this chapter, I do not wish to spend too long on the technicalities of assessment systems. I am interested in prompting you as teachers to think about the summative assessments you make and what they mean to the learners with whom you work. This may not be relevant to all the situations in which adults learn or is it? Even if your course does not have a compulsory concluding assessment of the learning, remember Jess. Before she felt ready to leave, she wanted some sense of closure and this may look a lot like asking for summative assessment. Those adult learning courses which provide certificates of attendance are providing the least demanding form of summative assessment ('You showed up'); this may represent a very considerable achievement for adults who have neither enjoyed nor succeeded in attempts to learn in the past. By way of contrast some assessments can totally dominate the learning so that only those activities which will have an obvious and direct impact on the assessment are valued by the participants. It is my firm conviction that assessment should support and anchor learning rather than distort it. Teachers may find this relatively easy to achieve in some contexts and much harder in others.

Border-crossings: assessment as 'citizenship'

The three purposes for assessment that we have already discussed are clearly part of the learning process: they are focused on identifying, communicating, affirming and improving what people can do. The idea of personal improvement lies at the heart of all three: it is implicit that learning is an activity open to all, and that its outcome will be progress towards expertise, proficiency, competence, virtuosity, or some other expression of accomplishment in the learner's chosen field. In assessment, we popularly claim to recognize and act upon changes in behaviour or performance when the learner is operating under certain conditions. As such, assessment is generally considered to be specific to a particular situation, and learners are not expected to infer that the outcome of the assessment reflects upon their character or accomplishments in general.

This fourth purpose for assessment is different, however. It demonstrates that assessment not only is concerned with assessing learning but also, in some circumstances, contributes to the selection of learners for benefits or sanctions. This distinction is worth reflecting upon for a moment. This function of assessment is often caught up with summative assessment, measuring and reporting the learning that has taken place. In other words in some circumstances we are not just judging if learning has happened (was Kevin able to sing any of the music after he had experienced being among the other basses as they were rehearsing and performing it?), we are also being asked, on the basis of past performance, to predict potential to improve. Assessors may be asked about the learner's potential (for example, could Kevin sing the same piece with just one or two other bass singers to sustain the part or could he tackle a harder work in big group?). I have described this predictive function as a 'border crossing' as it might afford or deny access to opportunity and responsibility as yet unimagined. This is the kind of assessment we are asked to undertake when we examine students in aspects of initial or continuing professional practice, audition village members to join local choirs, recommend FE college students for undergraduate study at university or interview applicants for a job. This kind of assessment is not about helping the learner to understand how they are doing and help them to improve. It is about all sorts of other things. Depending on your perspective, you might look upon the role in different ways. Those ways might include:

- Including or excluding people from groups, professions and opportunities
- Safeguarding the public from charlatans, imposters and incompetents
- Protecting privilege
- Widening participation and encouraging access
- Rationing scarce resources
- Defining boundaries.

This is controversial as well as technically difficult. It requires us to articulate our own understanding of professional ethics and personal values since its implications can resonate some long way away from the location of the learning which we have assessed. Nonetheless, it is a responsibility which is placed upon many teachers of adults.

Assessing learning requires both teachers and learners to make informed judgements on the basis of sound criteria. We need to act with integrity, precision and compassion. We need to have confidence that when scrutinized by those equipped to do so, our decisions will be recognized as consistent and fair. We intend them to motivate learners to persist with learning and enable them to make the most efficient use of their effort and often the cash they pay in fees. In order to achieve this we need to be alert to sources of bias in ourselves and our learners. Let us think about these issues next.

A typology of individual difference: how can it help with assessment?

The various purposes outlined earlier illustrate that the vast majority of assessment – and certainly those parts which most impact upon the learning process – is ultimately concerned with conveying information (feedback) to the learner. People vary, however, in the way that they choose to give feedback and in how they prefer to receive it.

An understanding of personality type can help a teacher in giving (and receiving) feedback constructively. A 'theory of personality' is merely an attempt to identify and explain differences and similarities between people in a systematic way: Freud's psychoanalytic theory, for example, applied a developmental model and famously gave new consideration to the impact of the unconscious. The field of personality theory is wide, although most modern influences stem from thinkers in the psychological and psychoanalytic traditions (some key figures are introduced in Chapter 5). Jung's model, which is the basis for a typology of individual difference, sits between theories which assume that people can be treated as if what they have in common is more important than any particular differences (such as behaviourism or cognitive developmentalism) and those which think that each person's learning is unique (such as constructivism) (see Chapters 1 and 2).

Jung's work is not often included in overviews of educational theory. I include it because his typology provides the basis for the Myers Briggs Type Indicator (MBTI) ®, an instrument which can be used to help people understand their psychological preferences and how those preferences might influence communication, problem solving, conflict resolution, career and personal life choices, and, of course, the ways they prefer to learn (and teach). Kolb's (1984) influential work on experiential learning (which draws upon work by the theorists Piaget, Lewin and Dewey) also refers to Jung. The clear practical application of some aspects of Jung's thinking (and its emphasis on personal recognition of preference rather than on the 'external' analysis of experts) makes it especially powerful in the context of education and professional development. It has certainly helped me greatly in my professional practice, not only equipping me to understand myself (and thus exert a greater degree of conscious control over the way in which I give feedback) but also in articulating a theoretical framework in which to consider the potential needs of particular learners. As such, Jung's theory of psychological type is of considerable use as a 'practical theory' for teachers wishing to improve their assessment practice.

The following pages introduce Jung's theory in more detail and consider its application through the MBTI. This brief introduction leads to some practical conclusions on assessment, and will hopefully provide a common language for further debate and study.

Jung's theory of personality

Jung's classic (although difficult, and at times contradictory) work on personality was published in 1921, even though it was not translated into English for another 50 years. His approach to the understanding of human personality was derived, in part, from observation of healthy subjects. His theory includes a concern with the conscious elements of the personality which he considered to be 'structured by four preferences concerning the use of perception and judgement' (Jung 1971: 8).

People are observed to have a set of mental tools with which they work. These tools or functions are used to access or attend to information (perception) and to make decisions about it (judgement). Although everyone has access to the same set, individuals are born with a tendency towards preferences in their use. These preferences, sometimes called habits of mind, represent the cognitive choices which an individual will tend to make when no stronger learned influence is acting upon their thinking. In contemporary terms, they represent a 'default setting' to which the individual personality will tend to return. Working within one's preferences tends to improve confidence and boost mental 'energy'; working outside them for sustained periods can do the opposite.

Jung identified opposite processes for each function. He thought that everyone is likely to use all four mental functions on some occasions, but that people vary both in their preference for one of the processes comprising each function and their consistency in doing so. His model is a sophisticated one, but we can consider a brief summary here.

One means of perception is the process of *sensing* (relying primarily on information received through the five physical senses, placing great value on practical experience); its opposite is *intuition* (characterized by an attention more to apparent patterns than detail, an inclination to making hypotheses before gaining evidence, an orientation to future possibility rather than present impressions). When making a judgement an individual might prefer to rely on the *thinking* process (characterized by rationality, consistency, objectivity, a concern for justice and a degree of detachment) or its opposite, *feeling* (characterized by an appraisal of values underlying decisions and consequences, concern for the exceptions to a rule, preference for decisions which promote harmony regardless of strict logic). Despite the terminology, both 'thinking' and 'feeling' processes are cognitive; both are concerned with making a 'reasoned' judgement, albeit reflecting different priorities.

These two functions (perception and judgement) do not, however, exist in isolation: two other factors affect their use. First, people vary in their relative interest in their 'inner' (relating to thoughts, depth and contemplative space) and 'outer' (relating to the material, physical environment of people and things) worlds: Jung introduced the terms *introversion* and *extraversion* to describe these different processes. Second, people tend to vary in their preferred way of responding to the world, being either inclined to 'jump in' or to hang back and 'observe' before engaging. Jung also expressed these concepts (somewhat confusingly for this simple summary) by the terms *judging* and *perceiving*. As Myers and Myers put it:

> One more preference enters into the identification of type – the choice between the perceptive attitude and the judging attitude as a way of life, a method of dealing with the world around us. Although people must of course use both perception and judgement, both cannot be used at the same moment . . . most people find one attitude more comfortable than the other, feel more at home in it and use it as often as possible when dealing with the outer world.
>
> (Myers and Myers 1995: 8)

It is important to note that Jung's theory does not suggest that any particular set of preferences ('a type', in MBTI terms) is 'better' than any other set, or that individuals are unable to operate effectively outside their preferences. Instead, his theory acknowledges that people *can* operate within the context of any of the processes (and, through practice in particular situations, can become more comfortable in doing so) but, when all else is equal, they are *more likely* to rely on their preferred ones. People will generally operate most efficiently (achieving the greatest output for the least expended effort) when they work in their preferred ways. For our present purposes, Jung's model offers a useful way of appreciating diversity of thought in both learners and teachers.

Applying Jung's theory: the Myers Briggs Type Indicator ®

Jung's analysis of personality has been widely exploited in the United States through its development into the MBTI. Interest in the instrument is growing worldwide; it has now been translated into more than 20 languages. Widely used for professional development, I have found it to be a powerful tool when applied to education, and especially the formation and development of teachers.

Isabel Briggs Myers' story is an inspiring one for adult learners in its own right. Considering the problems faced by women in the United States of the 1940s, required to work in 'men's' occupations while the men served in the armed forces, Myers wondered whether it would be possible to use Jung's theories (of which she initially had only a passing knowledge) to obtain a better fit between individual women and the work to which they were assigned. Sharing in work initiated by her mother Katharine Cook Briggs (and overcoming considerable difficulties caused by their amateur status), they developed an approach to assisting people to identify what Myers termed their 'best selves'. This approach grew into the MBTI, a tool whose influence has been far greater than could have been predicted from its humble origins.

The MBTI assists adults in recognizing, for themselves, their psychological preferences. By means of a questionnaire, supported in its interpretation by an MBTI-registered practitioner, a user can identify their own preferences, and apply such knowledge to a range of professional and personal contexts. Preferences are organized into a dynamic psychological type, reflecting four opposite processes (Extraversion/Introversion, Sensing/Intuition, Thinking/Feeling, Judging/Perceiving). The type is *dynamic* because it recognizes that the whole personality is more than the sum of the parts identified to aid analysis. This model is not restrictive: adults can (although, for various reasons, may not) act effectively when acting with or against their preferences. The MBTI is based on a substantial body of empirical research, underpinning the reliability and validity of the questionnaire. (Further information can be found in the excellent introductory work by Myers and Myers 1995.)

If you are interested, you should take steps to obtain a feedback with a registered practitioner. Details may be available from your place of work, or via the publishers licensed to distribute MBTI materials in your home country. Material purporting to be based on the MBTI is widely available over the Internet but it may not be reliable and should be approached with caution.

Some implications of individual difference for assessment

Teachers with an appreciation of their own preferences (especially with regard to the perceiving and judging functions) will be able to recognize how their own personality may affect their approach to assessment. The judging and perceiving functions exert a powerful influence on what an individual tends to notice, what they use as a basis for decisions and how those decisions are made. These activities are integral to the assessment process. Differences in personality may thus account, at least in part, for preferred ways of assessing and being assessed. Different teachers may attend to different information and/or decide about its importance on the basis of different personal approaches.

An understanding of personality preference helps to ensure that decisions about assessment are informed by professional considerations, rather than the personality of the teacher. As the most basic example, teachers with a personal preference for sensing and thinking may attribute greater value to forms of assessment which emphasize the readily quantifiable assessment of experience (including 'traditional' forms of summative assessment, like exams); teachers with a preference for intuition and feeling, however, may attribute greater value to forms of assessment tailored to the individual learner (such as portfolio submission) and recognizing more subjective achievements (distance travelled, and so on). As we have already noted, both of these forms and purposes of assessment (somewhat polarized for the purpose of the present example) are useful and valid. They do different things well and so are suitable for different purposes. Methods of assessment must be chosen because they are fit for purpose, not because an individual teacher personally prefers one or an other.

An awareness of preferences also offers, equally importantly, an insight into the differences between learners. Teachers know that assessment can be a surprising business, and that learners do not always perform in ways that might be anticipated from informal estimates of their performance in other contexts. This may partly be explained by the fact that the learner is operating within their preferences when 'performing' within the context of a normal class and operating outside their preferences when completing work for formal assessment, or vice versa. This line of thought also illustrates the truth that use of a particular form of assessment is likely to advantage some learners, and disadvantage others. In a large group, it is probable that various preferences will be represented. It is true that particular disciplines or professions sometimes attract a disproportionate constituency from certain personality types, but in these circumstances, the teacher should be even more on the alert for individuals whose preferences are different. In the most extreme circumstances, the feeling of isolation which stems from having an 'unusual' personality type within the context of a professional or disciplinary culture can be traumatic, and potentially damaging. These feelings may be brought to the surface in the context of assessment.

All things being equal, adult learners are likely (although not certain) to have developed techniques to cope with difficulties with assessment forms which run counter to their preferences. However, a wide range of other factors (see generally Chapter 5) will affect a learner's ability to do this effectively: when in a 'low energy' state, learners are likely to find working outside their preferences difficult. The stress of assessment may also affect this process.

An understanding of personality preferences also translates into a range of practical suggestions relating to assessment, as discussed in the following sections.

Bias

We should be aware of the potential for bias towards those learners who share our preferences. Communication may be easier to establish. There may be a sense of common understanding. Conversely, we may mistake attempts at clarification by learners with the opposite preference as challenges or negativity towards us or about the setting of learning tasks.

An appearance of gender bias in some situations may in fact result from a preference for or against the feeling process (rather than its thinking opposite). When writing descriptors or learning outcomes, or even selecting a form of assessment, we must be alert to a bias towards our own preferences.

Setting tasks and their interpretation

When preparing written instructions for assessments, it may be helpful to test them on someone with the opposite perceiving preference. Sensing types and intuitive types approach the task of writing instructions very differently. One is not better than the other. It is important to check, however, that instructions communicate precisely what they need to say to all who need to be able to follow them. Learners being assessed in a new way (e.g. one based on competence rather than academic knowledge) may be particularly concerned that the instructions provided for them are clear and precise.

Feedback

People who differ in their preferences are likely to interpret and respond to feedback in different ways. Without training, people tend to give feedback in the way they like to receive it. They can sometimes be mystified (and occasionally rather cross at the apparent waste of their time) when it appears not to achieve the intended impact. Even with training, giving feedback can remain a difficult activity: given the intimate play of individual character and preferences, it is hard to provide any hard and fast rules.

Ideally, in giving feedback, the teacher should try both to present it honestly (perceived integrity is generally valued highly by adult learners) and in a way which matches the preferences of the learner. Feeling types, for example, tend to be most comfortable when hearing positive aspects of feedback first, and constructive ('negative') aspects latterly, expressed as advice for improvement. Thinking types, on the other hand, may not expect – or be interested in – comment on what is 'good' (they may believe they already know that, and be more inclined to trust their own judgement in that regard than the teacher's); instead, they may be interested to see if the teacher has spotted any weaknesses of which they are not yet aware.

For obvious reasons, the giving of feedback represents something of a compromise: the degree to which the teacher can be true to their own style while meeting the needs of the learner may vary with each individual instance. Moreover, it is clear that the most effective feedback can generally only be given when the teacher and learner have a well-established relationship, with trust and sound acquaintance on both sides.

When this is not possible, the teacher should at least strive to reach a negotiated form of feedback with the learner, where both sides 'agree' (or at least understand) the rules by which the feedback will be given. Difficulty generally arises when there is ambiguity about the context in which feedback is given, its purposes, and its meaning.

The following anecdote illustrates how personality can easily come into play in a practical context. In particular, it highlights that even the use of modern 'good practice' conventions (commenting on success already achieved before highlighting what needs to be done for improvement) may still be misunderstood when the cognitive preferences of the actors involved are different.

Charlie, recently appointed as a new lecturer in a university, was a student on a compulsory module of professional development in teaching. He was very committed to his research and rather resentful of the time he had to spend working for this module.

About two-thirds of the way through, all participants on the module had been strongly advised to submit a draft of the portfolio on which they were to be assessed in order to receive formative feedback. Charlie duly did so. His tutor spent considerable time writing encouraging comment about the work to date and, as she had been taught, then added detailed comment on what still needed to be done to reach the pass required. At the conclusion of the module Charlie handed the portfolio in and was then enraged to discover that he had not passed. His anger was so extreme that neither the tutor nor the course leader could find a way to resolve the situation. The course leader finally proposed that I should read the portfolio and meet Charlie as an 'honest broker'.

I was not a little nervous when we were about to meet. However, within a few minutes the situation had become clear and the conflict easily resolved. It emerged in our discussion that when Charlie had started to read the feedback on his draft, he had misunderstood the convention of opening with a considerable amount of comment on positive aspects of the work so far, thinking it indicated that he had already reached the required standard. So, he had not bothered to read to the end and therefore he had not discovered that there were still substantial things he needed to amend or develop in order to pass. He believed, incorrectly but sincerely, that he had been advised that the portfolio would pass and so was very angry (and not a little humiliated) when it did not. The tutor had been very concerned about Charlie's inability to benefit from all the feedback she had provided for him and then became cross as he appeared too stubborn or lazy to do as she had suggested. In MBTI terms, Charlie prefers the thinking process, supported by intuition, while his tutor prefers the feeling process, supported by sensing. Neither had anticipated how the other could possibly see the situation in such a different way.

This story illustrates that there may be circumstances when even well intentioned and serious-minded individuals may misunderstand each other. It is not possible to ensure that this will never happen. An appreciation of differences in the way people can interpret a situation can help us to identify the source of a problem when it has occurred and take appropriate steps to limit the damage done.

Preparation for assessment

Discussing with adult learners how they learn, as well as what they learn, can help them to appreciate differences of approach. All types need to become aware of the benefits to be gained by working with all four processes, not just their preferred ones. An approach to problem solving (or preparing for assessment) which systematically includes sensing, intuition, feeling and thinking can aid learners to cover a topic more thoroughly and to present information in a way which will be recognized as effective by examiners of any type.

It is essential to remember that people tend to lack confidence in their performance when working with non-preferred processes, even if they have learned to do it well. Work outside preference is also more tiring and feels less comfortable. However, as with any activity, supported practice and training build familiarity, confidence and stamina. A rounded approach to teaching and assessment styles, suited to a variety of preferences, can also help to resituate learners in their own way of being, in much the same way as going on holiday can reintroduce the pleasures of being 'at home'. As one student reported:

> This [course] helped to reaffirm the trajectory of my own approach to learning and teaching – partly by offering alternative approaches which I could see were 'not me' and therefore would be problematic; and partly by allowing me time to reflect on, develop, and consolidate the ways in which I am happy to practise.
>
> (Student feedback)

Finally, it is important to realize that everyone procrastinates some-times! Awareness of psychological preferences helps to predict when we, and our learners, are most likely to do so. There is a tendency for those who prefer perceiving, for example, to delay completion of tasks, to need the last minute rush towards a deadline to motivate them. There is an expectation that some new information will generally turn up and a pre-disposition to welcome it when it does, and adapt work accordingly. Those who tend to deal with the external world by means of their judging pre-ference will often enjoy planning their lives. Usually, they will choose to organize their time (and that of those around them if possible) so that they can work towards a deadline in an orderly way, and ideally with time to spare. They will be unlikely to welcome distractions caused by new insights at the last minute and may experience grief if planned activity fails to occur. They may tend to put off relaxation, until work is done.

Both preferences have clear strengths and weaknesses. Teachers may find the apparent insouciance of those with perceiving preferences almost heart-stopping: the 'escape velocity' required for high performance in formal assessment may be very late to manifest itself to another person. It is hard for the teacher to recognize when a crisis is genuinely threatened, or when they are merely confronted with a personal style that they may not share. As illustrated by the account of Professor George and Julian's relationship earlier in this chapter, attempting to 'save' some-one with a perceiving preference from themselves may not be at all wel-come. Teachers of those with perceiving preferences need to recognize the autonomy and agency of the learner, while making sure that their own ability to help (and the parameters within which this is possible) is clearly understood. Although self-aware perceiving types are often good at meeting deadlines, they may tend to miss them dramatically when they make an error of judgement.

Learners with judging preferences may be more reassuring to the teacher in the run-up to assessment. They will often exhibit clear signs of their progress, and enable teachers to make a sound estimate of their degree of preparation. The relationship between teachers and learners with judg-ing preferences may be more challenging in other respects, however. Learners of this nature may not be comfortable when the progres-sion of the syllabus is less clear to them, and may be inclined to seek 'closure' too soon. This can be a particular problem when teaching 'softer' subjects, where the relationship between the learners and the course of study is more reflexive. Similarly, judging types may be concerned by assessment models actually designed to be more user-friendly. One form of assessment used on the MA course on which I teach is the portfolio, assembled from a variety of assignments that the learners undertake over the span of an entire module. This approach has the benefit of avoiding a 'single point of failure': rather than requiring participants to produce MA-level work on a given topic and at a given instance, they have a sustained opportunity to do so in a variety of contexts. This is not an easier option – the portfolio must still reflect MA-level thinking over all – but they have greater flexibility in how and when they do it. Nonetheless, despite explanation of this reasoning, a number of learners with judging preferences often report some difficulty in coping with the required open-endedness. One has observed to me:

> I had some difficulty understanding what some elements of the portfolio were asking me to do . . . I feel that individual items in the assessment might be made clearer if followed by an explanation of what is 'acceptable' in each, perhaps linked more specifically to the descriptors.
>
> (Student feedback)

Again, neither teacher nor learner is 'wrong'. When working in such contexts (i.e. those where the learners' capacity to interpret the task is an aspect of it) extra care must be taken to ensure that everyone understands the particularities of such assessment. An appreciation of psychological type assists in the avoidance of basing important decisions on the assumption that other people think the way we do.

Two contemporary issues in assessment

The theory of psychological preference is a useful tool for analysing and developing much of assessment practice. However, it also highlights a small number of assessment issues to which it is not easily suited. Two of these issues, both highly relevant to contemporary practice with adults, are competence-based assessment and group assessment. Of themselves conceptually distinct, they are united in the way they tend to displace individual personality from the centre of the teacher's attention in designing assessment.

Competence-based assessment tends to value consistent performance of specific outcomes under controlled conditions, an approach to which personality is formally irrelevant. Its guiding principle is the idea of its own objectivity. (In fact, however, this approach may sit more easily with some personality types than others. Nonetheless, the object of competence-based assessment is consistency rather than the true reflection of the nuances of individual performance.)

Group assessment may not just be the assessment of multiple individual learners. Instead, it may involve the assessment of a distinct entity:

'the group' rather than the sum of the participating individuals. As such, the 'personality' of the entity is not straightforwardly rooted in the psychology of the individuals but also in social dynamics; the behaviour of groups may reflect the predominance of the preferences exhibited by certain members. These may, of course, vary with time and shifts in personal influence.

We shall briefly consider each of these issues in turn.

Competence-based assessment

What do we mean by competence? The Working Group on Vocational Qualifications defined it as 'the ability to do a particular activity to a prescribed standard' (WGVQ 1986: 59, cited in Tight, 2002). It is, however, inevitably bound up with a range of other notions, reflected in the fuller definition offered by the Unit for the Development of Adult Continuing Education (UDACE 1989):

> *Competence is concerned with what people can do rather than with what they know.* This has several implications:
>
> *Firstly*, if competence is concerned with doing then it must have a *context* . . .
>
> *Secondly*, competence is an *outcome*; it describes what someone can do. It does not describe the learning process which the individual has undergone . . .
>
> *Thirdly*, in order to measure reliably someone's ability to do something, there must be clearly defined and widely accessible *standards* through which performance is measured and accredited;
>
> *Fourthly*, competence is a measure of what someone can do at *a particular point in time*.
>
> (UDACE 1989: 6, emphasis supplied)

We should take a moment to unpack some of these ideas. Measuring what people can *do* is an important function for a great deal of learning. Adults often enter into education with a practical purpose in mind: they want to plumb a house, drive a car, sing in a choir, swim underwater, fly an aeroplane, treat an ill person to make them better, and so on. Success in these pursuits is best measured in practical terms: can the learner demonstrate their ability to complete the required task? In the case of some of these activities, however, the learner's ability to complete the task once in the assessment may not be sufficient guarantee: 'safety critical' activities such as driving, flying and surgery (to varying extents) require a higher indication of probability that the learner can consistently complete the relevant activities satisfactorily. It is at this point that the notion of competence-based assessment becomes more challenging. Although the model was initially intended to simplify the assessment process somewhat, even a brief examination of the context of the competence raises questions about consistency (particularly with regard to the passage of time, and the influence of changing conditions) and thus the extent to which a demonstrated competence is a useful outcome of learning.

Competence-based systems of assessment gained a high profile during the 1980s and 1990s, initially as a political response to a perceived need to retrain and up-skill the workforce at a time of relatively high unemployment in a post-industrial economy at low cost to employers. Deliberately or otherwise, the new scheme was largely drawn up by individuals from government and the private sector, and seemed to lack input from the existing educational community. Whatever its cause, one consequence of this policy was the gap which quickly developed between 'academic' and 'vocational' spheres of education and training in England. It is worth noting that this gap (which, to a certain extent, continues today) is unhelpful, and to be regretted. The two traditions have different strengths, and could have been designed to articulate properly from the start. Despite much talk of 'ladders' and 'bridges', there is still a practical separation that is very hard to overcome. Competence-based assessment, developed and rolled out in the light of the needs of the business community, acquired the reputation as a straightforward tool sufficient to do the job. Although this is true to a point, it is important to note that it has limitations as a model, and does not avoid many of the problems associated with other forms of assessment.

The most extensive competence-based system of assessment in England is the National Vocational Qualification (NVQ). Its development began with an analysis of the occupations for which people required qualifications, broken down to reveal the functions and activities each job comprised, and taking into account varying levels of seniority. This analysis was then used as the basis for devising a system of assessment (organized into discrete units) intended to match occupational requirements and be carried out in the workplace if possible by direct observation of working practice at a time when individuals judged themselves to be ready. This process could work reasonably well for small occupational communities, whose members were in regular contact with one another, and thus whose practices were reasonably cohesive. However, in attempting to apply the system on a national scale, it became clear that different standards of practice prevailed in different places. The system therefore required people to be trained as assessors and also as verifiers to ensure that assessment systems were implemented consistently right across the country. Despite the fact that this increased the cost of assessment, there are many competence-based vocational qualifications operating currently.

Let us look at a straightforward example of where it might work very well and then touch on more challenging contexts. If you are training people to work on the Virgin west coast mainline as train managers, it makes sense that the competence they develop should enable them to work on one of the other Virgin lines or indeed with minimal company-specific orientation, for any other train company. Much of the skill (another slippery concept) which is judged as competent is alleged to be transferable. For example, customer care is roughly the same whether you are travelling from Euston to Birmingham or from St Pancras to York . . . or is it? All but the most straightforward of tasks vary from one situation to another. Competence systems are great to check if people are broadly effective at what they have to do most of the time and under most conditions. They cannot be used to develop potential to move beyond the current boundaries of the job. Where complex (higher level) competence is required, for example management development or counselling, even the NVQ system seems to mix the pure competence-based system with approaches and techniques drawn from academic practice, traditional apprenticeships, reflective practice, and so on. This is for a number of reasons including:

- The complexity and sometimes controversial nature of the initial functional analysis upon which a notion of competence is based.
- Direct observation is the most reliable evidence for assessment of competence; this becomes problematic where the occupation requires considerable thought, professional judgement or is conducted in a confidential environment.
- Underpinning knowledge and understanding normally require 'academic' assessment.

Finally, before we leave competence-based assessment, learning to scuba dive provides an example of the ways in which human differences can affect competence-based systems as much as any other forms of assessment. The Professional Association of Diving Instructors (PADI) system for training and assessment of competence is highly regarded. It has worldwide recognition and is rigorous in its attention to detail, regulation of accredited centres and provision of materials and resources. It is in all respects an example of best practice in this type of assessment. However, even here firsthand knowledge of two different diving schools, both PADI registered, provide examples of serious differences in their approach to learning. This is a cautionary tale, although with a happy ending.

Both schools adhered precisely to the rules and regulations laid down for the training and conduct of assessment but they differed in the quality and attitude of the instructors themselves. In one situation, the instructors were not able or apparently interested in recognizing that different novice divers needed to be encouraged and motivated appropriately to build confidence and enjoyment of the training. They were primarily motivated to complete courses leading to assessment for which they were paid, irrespective of the success or failure of the trainees. I started my training with such an organization, unable to detect initially that they would show so little concern for me once I had paid for the course. Looking back now I realize that there were indicators that the training was not as good as it could have been, but as a novice it was hard for me to tell at the time.

I was much older than the other participants and I was not included in any of the social activity associated with membership of the class. After some weeks, the instructors told me that I had to take the assessment of competence in open water, in a wetsuit, in February.

The water was so cold that I couldn't control my breathing enough to even begin the assessment of underwater skills. With my confidence and self-esteem badly shaken and having used up all my cash, I gave up and thought I would never qualify as an open water diver.

Some months later a friend who dives regularly suggested I should take one more lesson with the school which had trained her. Very scared and rather cynical about the whole business, I agreed. Kate, my new instructor, was extraordinary. She treated me with a respect and concern I had not previously enjoyed. She quickly built my confidence. Without being overtly critical of my former instructors, she indicated it was not the only occasion on which she had assisted novice divers to recover from poor experience. She accurately predicted that three classes with her would be sufficient for me to regain my confidence, be retrained in some key competences and pass the initial open water assessment. It was hugely satisfying to do so.

(Personal journal entry)

This example features an activity which is very well suited to the assessment of competence. Even where assessment in this way is appropriate and a programme of instruction has been designed to meet the standards required, the instructors still have to implement the programme in a way which does not discriminate against any of the participants. They must also ensure that the assessment is undertaken in suitable conditions rather than at the convenience of the instructors. If payment is triggered by the completion of the assessment there may be a temptation to neglect the best interests of participants. Competence-based schemes may look attractive to potential funders, for example where large numbers of people need to be trained to a common standard. The organization contracted to run the assessment may then be tempted to meet the needs of the funder (in order to retain the business) and neglect the personal cost to participants who have not been adequately trained or properly assessed. As with many systems designed to encourage learning and measure achievement, in the hands of expert ethical teachers they work well and are fit for purpose.

Is group assessment ever really fair?

Life is not generally lived entirely in our own little bubbles. We can only accomplish some things by working together. The theoretical insights provided by the social constructivists illustrate this powerfully in learning. The emphasis on learning as a social activity requires interaction between individuals and mediation through face-to-face or distance techniques. Despite this growing recognition of the importance of the social, most summative assessment is still done as individuals. This is because it is very hard to get a group assessment which will deliver valid and reliable results with sufficient level of discrimination at a price we can afford. So, in most cases though the group can work well using peer feedback for formative assessment, it is not usually given a large role when leading to accredited performance. Participants who notice this, but do not understand the reasons, may be slow to respond well to the practice of peer feedback. The notion that only the teacher can tell you how you are getting on is very persistent. However, when students are taken carefully through an activity with peer feedback as a significant part of the process they realize that giving it as well as getting it can be a remarkable aid to learning for everyone. This is an important issue as it can, when used ethically, reduce time spent on marking by teachers. I am not proposing that they devote less time to the whole activity of teaching, I am saying that there is probably a better use of the time available.

There is also considerable pressure in the work-based learning contexts to assess people's ability to work together effectively in groups. By this I mean that the ability to undertake projects in groups and reach a successful conclusion is something about which employers for example want information on learners. So the business of designing an assessment which will accurately do this is also a challenge which some teachers need to meet.

Even before the assessment takes place, the process of forming the groups can impact on the learners. There are lots of ways groups can be formed and there is no correct approach. First, my best advice is that the worst thing you can do is either assign people without telling them why or leave it entirely to chance. In either case something will go wrong for some people. Second, in my view there should not be a single opportunity to be assessed when working in groups. With the best intentions there are often groups which just do not work. If the outcome is going to have a significant influence on someone's future, a minimum of three assessments should be done with people grouped differently for each one. Less evidence than that is not likely to be valid or reliable. Third, it may be useful to include a personal reflective journal in the mix. Even if one or more of the group project falls apart, the participants can still demonstrate some understandings of process, their ability to own responsibility for the success or failure of the group, their appreciation of other people's contribution, some analysis of what caused the failure or success. Careful preparation for such reflective writing will also increase the chance that the projects will succeed. Finally, when setting the task for group assessment, there must be equal opportunity for all members of the group to achieve the full range of marks available. Put rather crudely, if only the 'leader' can actually do some of the activities for which credit is available, then the task is unfair to the rest of the participants.

This is a good moment to introduce a final word on the use of descriptors in assessment. They are very useful when assessing portfolios or other work which requires participants to choose their own way of undertaking the task and presenting the outcome. Descriptors clearly signal to the participant and the examiners how the credit is to be earned. In other words they describe what must be done to succeed. Typically they can be quite tight if you want individual learners to really concentrate on specific outcomes or they can be more loosely defined to give latitude for personal interpretation within a framework. When undertaking group assessment they are even more essential. Carefully written descriptors (which the groups can discuss and check differences of interpretation with a teacher) significantly improves student learning by developing their understanding of assessment criteria and processes (Rust et al. 2003).

Conclusions and summary

If I had 15 minutes of your time to talk about assessment with you, how should we spend it? I am going to list the headlines:

- Assessment of learning is a key professional competence for teachers.
- 'How am I doing?' This is the key question for learners.
- Facing judgements about ourselves and our performance in activities which matter to us can be very scary.
- Teachers build confidence in their learners by structuring appropriate challenges and providing commentary on the way we tackle them.
- Learners acquire a mental map of the territory as a result of those exchanges with their teacher, themselves and their peers and through doing so begin to be able to identify the degree of difficulty of a challenge and whether they are up to the task for themselves (see Chapter 6).
- Past experience (for good or ill) impacts on current confidence.
- Learners and teachers build trust in each other. This can be compromised when the learner fears that the teacher is acting in the interests of a third party, that is, is assessing them in order to report to somebody else who has power over them how good or bad they are.
- When teachers are assessing learning in the interests of an organization or individual, they have become 'examiners' or 'selectors'. Such roles bring particular responsibilities and at the very least learners must not be confused by a conflict in roles.
- Assessment involves setting clear tasks in ways which can be understood by all participants and judging them in pre-agreed ways. They should be capable of moderation by a competent critical friend.
- Assessment for adults should generate no nasty surprises.
- Assessment should provide the building materials which enable adults to feel and behave in self-directing, autonomous responsible and enjoyable ways.
- Assessment can trigger unexpected and powerful anxiety; it can make us feel vulnerable, foolish and resentful (even when the teacher has done nothing wrong). In other words a learner's response to an assessment is not always rational.
- Summative assessment can prompt grief; for the ending of the course, separation from friends and teachers and/or for the work we were going to do and did not do.
- Every item of summative assessment can still be a starting point for the next learning challenge.

5 Positive approaches to participant wellbeing:
Social, environmental and emotional factors in teaching

Traditional pedagogy (cognitive or behaviourist, individual or social) tends to be serious stuff. It is undeniably important and an understanding helps considerably with course design, including the selection of methods, materials, activities and assessments. However, pedagogic theories are more or less silent about the warmth, humanity, excitement and misery which may also be part and parcel of the experience of teaching and learning. They are influences of which the teacher should be aware, if they are to be brought within some conscious control. In short, most cognitive or behavioural perspectives are less help when trying to appreciate how teaching or learning *feels*. Nor can they account for the significance of this feeling. Given the primary importance to learning of its various emotional aspects (especially, in the adult context, to motivation – why learn, why teach: all parties involved could be doing something else . . .), this 'gap' is not altogether helpful.

In this chapter, we will remedy this deficit by drawing on perspectives from the fields of psychoanalysis and humanistic psychology. These fields of study provide different theoretical lenses through which we can develop a framework to understand the emotional aspects of learning, including motivation, satisfaction of needs, origins of anxiety and sources of pleasure. Interestingly, the other major source of reflection in this area seems to originate in Hollywood: there is a wide range of films which provide informal explorations of teaching and learning – and, for dramatic purposes, they do not shrink from the emotional. They may provide an enjoyable companion to this chapter, and not nearly so far-fetched as you might think.

The chapter concludes with some practical suggestions about ways to energize and engage in teaching. You will be able to consider if any of them may be useful in the situation in which you work.

The relationship between cognitive and affective factors in learning

Abraham Maslow described his psychology as 'humanistic'. In the social and political context in which he lived and worked, he believed that it was the work of psychology to bring to light an underlying set of principles which might unify understanding of human personality. Although a scientist, much of his writing has a 'spiritual' quality. He made a substantial contribution to a model which worked towards a common understanding of human needs and their influence on behaviour.

In his work, we see some of the origins of the abundance models of teaching and development. At best, motivation is not simply a matter of meeting the material needs of existence; human effort is applied in the solution of less mundane problems and towards creativity, philanthropy and fulfilment. Maslow believed his concept was potentially universal. It could be true of everyone and not just a privileged class, generation, colour or creed. Society had to ensure that the basic needs of all people were met so that they could progress towards the fulfilment of their innate potential. His work may be criticized as romantic idealism in a post-war environment, or as unduly influenced by American cultural aspirations or utopian visions. Regardless, Maslow has had a significant influence on the development of American psychology and of educational theory and practice.

Maslow is generally remembered for the outworking of this approach within a framework known as the hierarchy of needs, first encapsulated in a paper published in the United States in 1943. Such needs were described as being of two different kinds: 'deficiency needs' and 'being or meta needs'. He proposed that the most basic physiological requirements to sustain life generally had to be satisfied first, for example 'a person who is lacking food, safety, love and esteem would most probably hunger for food more strongly than for anything else' (Maslow 1970: 37).

There is considerable wisdom in Maslow's work (and it has been highly influential on and influenced by others who theorize adult learning) – as long as we are able to see it in context and not with a limiting or distorting rigidity. First, we can observe that, at a time when so many people were deprived of the most basic survival needs, it is not surprising that he articulated those as fundamental. Second, he believed that once the right to such fundamentals is established, everyone would be motivated towards satisfying their need for human affection and self-esteem. The idea of self-actualization, a concept which connotes much more than the basic requirements of a physical existence, epitomizes the aspirational nature of much adult learning; its position at the top of the hierarchy suggests that its effective realization is contingent upon adequate access to more 'basic' needs.

This truth is worth recalling in the context of the practicalities of the individual teaching encounter, as well as the learner's life in general. Teachers need to remember how hard it is to learn when one is cold, tired, hot or hungry. At its most fundamental, there are core physical requirements which must be satisfied before most people can concentrate effectively on learning. The designers of many teaching spaces, or those with responsibility for scheduling opportunities for teaching or professional development sometimes appear to forget this. They do so at their (and our) peril. More generally, it is something of a truism to acknowledge that success in learning corresponds (at least in a statistical sense) to economic, social, political and domestic equilibrium.

Maslow's hierarchy may be subject to criticism, especially if one seeks to apply it prescriptively. It remains entirely possible for individual learners to overcome the limitations of even severely adverse circumstances, and no theory of teaching should be used to deny that. Indeed, witnessing – or even contributing to – achievements of this nature often represents the highlight of a teacher's career. Maslow shows, however, that the probability of this occurring is low; his model is particularly effective as an expression of trends and probabilities, rather than as an absolute truth. Limitations in access to basic necessities make it harder for effective learning to take place until the deficiency is resolved. By inference, the teacher – not formally present in the hierarchy – could be defined as a compensating agent, potentially able to assist in 'beating the odds'.

The notion of self-actualization was a part of Maslow's (1968) broader appreciation (in his terms) of the 'psychology of being'. Rooted in cognitive psychology, he was distinctive for his sense of what he described as the 'transpersonal' and the 'transhuman'. He recognized that, under certain circumstances (which he came to describe as 'peak experiences'), it is possible to achieve a heightened sense of engagement by being true to one's own nature yet (simultaneously, and somewhat paradoxically) transcending it. Strange though this idea may sound on first acquaintance, it nonetheless seems an apt description for the epitome of the teaching experience.

Carl Rogers was an American therapist who became interested in learning; his writing was considerably influenced by Maslow and his colleagues. An alternative to psychoanalytic therapy, the counselling process (Rogers 1969; Rogers and Freiberg 1994) encourages people to fulfil their potential by a non-directive approach. This approach may be encapsulated in three principles to guide the professional relationship:

- Non-possessive warmth
- Accurate empathy
- Unconditional positive regard.

Apparently easy, it can be surprisingly hard to do, particularly if practitioners have previously been trained in didactic methods or as an instructor.

This approach has found its way into teaching practice in what are normally understood as facilitative methods. Teachers working in this way, unfortunately often without any significant relevant training, are expected to be able to manage groups in a non-directive way and so encourage learning through a process of action and reflection. Facilitation requires the teacher to live out the belief that adult learners have an abundance of relevant knowledge and experience. As such, facilitation rarely includes direct instruction (telling the learner what to do or how to do it). Instead, learners may require enabling or empowering in order to see for themselves the options they have and the ways in which they might carry them out. In certain circumstances, the teacher or facilitator's role may extend to negotiating specific interventions, processes or resources to assist in the planned response to the learning challenge. Learning will occur as the learners take responsibility for their own actions, reviewing the outcome and adjusting their behaviour accordingly.

If you talk to adults for whom learning is not associated with the pleasure of success, you may find stories of situations in which one or more of the three elements listed above was missing from the learning relationship. The emphasis on taking personal responsibility is shared with psychoanalytic practice. The difference lies in how it is achieved. Different situations may benefit from different approaches.

It is useful to comment here on the boundaries between teachers and therapists, and the different professional responsibilities engaged. Teaching can benefit from insights derived from counselling and therapy but it remains a distinct and separate process. In particular, the aims, responsibilities, ethics and professional development practices of teachers are different. One key distinction is that, while most therapists and counsellors are 'supervised', teachers are not. By this, I do not mean that teachers operate without accountability, but, unlike those working in a therapeutic environment, they are not required to be in therapy (or an analogous relationship) as a condition of their ongoing practice. This absence of a professional safety net for the teacher means that (for their own welfare) they must be scrupulous in not assuming professional responsibility for the learner beyond the scope of the learning relationship. As a corollary, the basis under which adults enter a learning situation is not the same as the psychosocial contract implied by a therapeutic relationship. Teachers, even using facilitative methods or other techniques informed by psychological perspectives, should be careful not to expect (much less demand) more from learners than is appropriate to a teacher–learner relationship. Feelings of ambush or trespass (into inappropriate roles such as parent or counsellor) can embarrass, disturb, intimidate or ultimately exclude the learner, obviously to the detriment of the learning process. It is thus particularly important to recognize, mark and conform to the appropriate professional boundary. If teachers encounter issues which require professional help beyond the limit of their competence, they are ethically obliged to suggest this (with appropriate tact) and offer to assist with referral. In certain activities (such as tutoring, supervising, mentoring, coaching or advising an action-learning set), the boundary between professional roles may be harder to discern – and for this reason, additional professional development should normally be undertaken to support these forms of practice.

The duty of care is paramount to the ethical responsibilities of both teachers and therapists, but its implications may differ. For example, although teachers should respect confidentiality, they are also obliged to seek appropriate assistance if a situation progresses beyond their experience and qualification and in so doing places learners at risk. Teachers must, of course, also respect all relevant legal obligations, such as the Data Protection Act 1998 and the Special Educational Needs Discrimination Act (SENDA) 2002 in the UK.

The work of Howard Gardner is also relevant to any exploration of the subtleties of interplay between the cognitive and affective elements in teaching and learning. Gardner (2006) writes one of a series of books in which experts in the field of education compile a collection of their major publications. The chapter entitled 'Beyond the IQ: Education and Human Development' revisits work first published in the *Harvard Education Review* in 1987. Gardner proposed 'a pluralistic view of the mind' (Gardner 2006: 48). He challenged the prevailing 'uniform view' proposing that intelligence might better be understood to be 'the ability to solve problems or to fashion products that are valued in one or more cultural settings' (Gardner 2006: 48). His ideas gained considerable support. They came to be known as a theory of 'multiple intelligences'. The original list included seven intelligences that Gardner and his colleagues had located through a wide-ranging survey of diverse and perhaps controversial range of sources. He characterized them as linguistic, logical-mathematical, spatial, musical, bodily-kinesthetic, interpersonal and intrapersonal (Gardner 2006).

Now almost a commonplace, this was a significant and contested approach when there was strong support for notions of a single unified intelligence, straightforwardly measurable by intelligence quotient (IQ) tests (first developed by Binet in Paris in 1900). The '11+ exam' (or its local equivalent), used to determine the type of secondary education for which a child was eligible, illustrates the result of pre-Gardner thinking, and its effect. Using verbal, numerical and mental reasoning components as the measure of ability, it served to stigmatize many children – and relegate them to an education from which it was hard to recover. Very few of those who failed the 11+ went directly into HE at 18; yet the successful performance in HE of these same individuals as mature students has demonstrated that there was no innate and unalterable lack of the necessary ability. A narrow conception of intelligence, as exemplified by the 11+, thus fails to provide useful guidance for educational decision-making. Gardner's work, recognizing diverse expressions of cognitive ability (which can be reorganized in a variety of appropriate ways), has opened up issues of selection, provision, assessment and specialization. These are relevant both to initial and continuing education.

Daniel Goleman's (1995) work took Gardner's thinking and made a significant media splash with the idea of 'emotional intelligence'. In doing so he privileged another single manifestation of intelligent thinking as important for the effective conduct of adult life. The emotional intelligence quotient (EQ) included both *intra*personal and *inter*personal perspectives. Goleman's work has been applied most extensively in particular cultural contexts but like Gardner it can be argued that while the specific manifestations will vary, the basic cognitive ability is relevant cross-culturally.

All four theorists discussed in this chapter so far (Maslow, Rogers, Gardner, Goleman) provide different kinds of evidence which point towards the potential benefits of working within an abundance model of adult learning. Working from an essentialist perspective (in other words, describing in universal terms what it means to be an adult human) their work highlights the complexity of the role that cognitive factors play in teaching and learning. In other words, they are representative of theorists who focus on individual differences in cognitive functioning. Some of the implications of Jung's ideas about psychological type (see Chapters 4 and 6) also contribute to the point being argued here. It is that teaching is much more than structuring and presenting content for transmission. Teaching is an active engagement in a dynamic relationship between people and the object of study in order for meaning to be made. This takes into account the comprehension of the material to be learned and the processes of learning which are optimized for specific learners. Such processes are influenced by cognitive and affective factors which combine to manifest themselves in thinking, feeling and behaving as learners.

Teachers of adults conceptualize their work differently in the light of the needs of particular students, situations or constraints. Viewed in this light, it becomes impossible to see learners only as 'empty vessels' waiting to be filled by a teacher with relevant knowledge to impart. Similarly, the idea that any professional teacher can be both competent and entirely non-learner-centred is challenged by this understanding.

As discussed in Chapter 1, recognition of the importance and the reality of the physical, cognitive and affective needs of learners does not, however, mandate the complete subjugation of the teacher. Rather, attention to the needs (broadly conceived) of learners is one perspective which the teacher must include in their general survey of their intended teaching practice.

A comprehensive study of theorists concerned with the needs of learners as an influence on teaching could occupy an entire book in itself: the four presented earlier, although important as an introduction to the key ideas, by no means represent the entire field. Not least is it important to note that once the influence of the cognitive is recognized more fully, *social* as well as individual factors must be taken into account. More than two centuries ago, Mary Wollstonecraft criticized the discrimination inherent in the thinking of Jean-Jacques Rousseau who, while a liberal reformer and early proponent of child-centred education for boys, failed to recognize the educational needs of girls. Wollstonecraft's early articulation of feminist thinking was nevertheless insufficient to remedy the problem which, to a certain extent, persists today (see further Belenky 1986; Gilligan 1982; Gore 1993). On a social, political and economic basis, the writer Paolo Freire (1996) has similarly explored the relevance of education to 'the oppressed' members of society, and its potential to aid or hinder their bid to free themselves.

An acknowledgement of feminist and other critiques also illustrates another theme which must be considered when we consider teaching and learning in this 'holistic' manner: what is the true basis upon which we found our ideas of education? Although, on the one hand, the essentialist writings of the humanistic psychologists help to underline the human attributes and requirements that must affect educational practice, anti-essentialist perspectives (some radical and feminist ones for example) caution that similar sweeping assertions can marginalize or exclude certain groups. In appreciating that teaching and learning is not simply a cognitive process, it is important to remain open-minded and reflective about the factors that may also be relevant, and not (accidentally or deliberately) impose new socially constructed rules under the mantle of objective truth.

Jack Mezirow's writings on transformative learning bring many of these themes together. In his analysis, he explicitly identifies the purpose of transformative learning as the recognition of limiting, discriminatory and anti-democratic habits of mind, points of view, and frames of reference so that they may be transformed into ones which will lead to the higher ideals of democracy (Mezirow and Associates 2000).

What does this all mean in practice? First, it is important to acknowledge that (palatable or not) many people do hold essentialist beliefs on some or all issues. Although teachers should be respectful of learners' opinions, there is some role for teachers to present appropriate stimuli and support for critical engagement with beliefs in appropriate settings. Second, obviously, teachers should beware of essentialist overtones in their own practice; although hard to completely avoid, reflective practice should assist in safeguarding that they do not adversely affect the learning process. Third, this thinking underlines the social role that teaching and learning have to play.

Fear and fun in the classroom

Alongside the direct impact of cognitive factors upon the learning process, the relationships (generally, teacher–learner and learner–learner) which occur within it also generate a significant emotional reaction. Both as children and adults, almost all of us can recall moments of boredom, amusement, interest, fun, worry and even terror engendered in the course of learning. These reactions can either impede or enhance the process, and must be taken seriously. Although affecting individual learners differently, it is important to remember that they are not beyond the teacher's control. Positive and negative emotional reactions can be handily encapsulated in the ideas of 'fear' (impeding learning) and 'fun' (assisting learning). It should be noted, however, that no emotional reaction is entirely positive or negative: a degree of apprehension can, depending on the circumstances, heighten or impair performance; fun can distract the learner's attention or assist them in attaining a state of 'flow' (see Chapter 6).

In exploring ideas of fear and fun in the classroom, it is particularly useful to refer to Salzberger-Wittenberg et al.'s *Emotional Experience of Learning and Teaching* (1999). I would wholeheartedly recommend the relevant part (73 pages) in its entirety for a good basic introduction to this area.

Though much of the theory relating to adult learners accurately describes that they can be grown-up, self-directing, autonomous and rational, Salzberger-Wittenberg et al. (1999) demonstrate that this may not be true all the time, and offer some explanation of the reasons for this. Insights along these lines are particularly important for us as teachers as they help us to understand why learners do not always behave as we might predict. As well as being experts in content and method, teachers should be able to make considered critical interventions into the learning situation (which is governed by social, environmental and emotional factors), and in so doing inspire confidence in their own roles as guardians of the learning process.

In considering the elements of teaching in Chapter 1, I included some brief advice about beginnings. Although the comments may have seemed rather basic, the importance of the beginning cannot be overemphasized. In many ways, beginnings are one of our most emotionally vulnerable points: both hopes and fears are sharply drawn. Without hope, we are rarely motivated to overcome inertia and to take a step forward; at the same time, the sense of forward movement makes many of us anxious, either through fear we will not like the new environment in which we find ourselves, or that we will prove ourselves to be inadequate to the challenge. Psychoanalytic theory suggests why such feelings are complex: in principle more or less universal to humans, they may also be culturally influenced and unique to us as individuals.

Providing even a brief encapsulation of psychoanalytic theory is a daunting task. However, for our purposes, one key idea ('transference') will give a flavour of the contribution this branch of theory can make to teaching. Salzberger-Wittenberg et al. define it in the following manner:

> Freud called this phenomenon of the past being constantly revived in the present 'the transference.' The tendency to repeat past patterns of relating is a universal phenomenon and recurs in any important relationship. Freud came to the conclusion that no experience is ever lost, it remains stored in the mind and ready to be reawakened in any situation that resembles the past in some way.
>
> (Salzberger-Wittenberg et al. 1999: 33)

Writing about transference in the specific context of the start of learning, they continue:

> The young child who comes to school, the adult at college, has been patterned not by one sequence of inter-play between inner and outer events, but by myriads of them which will have gradually created a very individual and unique pattern of relationships in his mind. It is this internal picture of the world and the relationships between himself and others (as well as between others) which is transferred into the new situation . . . we do not need to unravel a person's past if we are to understand him. If we are observant, we can gain insight into his assumptions and beliefs from his behaviour and reactions to ourselves and others in the here and now. Awareness of the transference elements enables us to have some space to think about the nature of the relationship, to take a more objective view of it.
>
> (Salzberger-Wittenberg et al. 1999: 35–6)

It is highly likely that at the beginning of a course of study – or even an individual session – some or all of the people involved will be transferring feelings from their previous experience (Youell 2005). In some cases, these feelings can be positive. Indeed, in some cases the feelings will be not only positive but also conscious, as people may manage their new start by actively drawing upon relevant previous experience. At the same time, there are likely to be other emotional influences in the room, conscious to the individuals concerned or otherwise, which may contribute to anxiety, scepticism or even open hostility. For obvious reasons, these emotions will also have an impact on the learning process, certainly for those under their sway but potentially also for learners in the group. There is some truth in the idea that, when teaching, the teacher must engage not only with the learners in the room but also with every other teacher those learners have ever had. (It is for this reason, among others, that I have found the use of 'educational autobiographies' to be such a powerful tool when I begin to work with new adult learners.) Understanding the significance of transference enables us as teachers to be prepared to take calm, kind and firm control of the situation, and so contain it.

From this analysis, it will become clear that the teacher's ability to take control of the situation depends on two things: a certain deftness of touch in managing the social atmosphere and the classroom relationships, and an ability to observe and understand the behaviour of learners in such a way as to gain insights which can inform the management of the classroom. In both respects, it is important not only to be able to do it but also to be *seen* to be doing it, fostering confidence that the learning environment is a 'safe' space. Neither of these skills is easy to impart through a book, although it is true that possessing the second will generally lead to the first. Most effective teachers will develop these abilities through thoughtful and reflective practice.

Here is another anecdote to illustrate the way these abilities can work.

Bernie, an MA student, was required to make a ten-minute presentation to her peers. Her peers, benefiting from the content of the presentation, would provide verbal feedback on substance and delivery. She would also receive written feedback on her presentation from two examiners which, with the presented material itself, would contribute to summative assessment. All the students in Bernie's group were scheduled to make their presentations on the same day, and this had been discussed on several occasions in previous learning sessions. They had also been given the date in writing many weeks before.

The day came. In order to complete the presentations for all members of the group on the same day, I had arranged to run two sessions in parallel, requiring double the normal space and equipment, and the presence of four examiners (including myself). Three suitably qualified colleagues had kindly made space in their own teaching schedules to serve in this capacity.

Five minutes before the session was scheduled to begin, Bernie took me to one side, and told me that she was very sorry but that she was not ready to do the presentation. She had got the date wrong, and had not done the preparation she thought necessary. Looking at her carefully, I was aware that I was faced with a difficult decision. Given my normal, flexible style of teaching, she clearly expected that I would agree to her request, and make arrangements for her to meet her obligation in some other way. At the same time, I knew that granting her request would disrupt the schedule of activities which would prepare her – and others in the group – for final assessment, cause her to be overworked in order to do the necessary 'catching-up' while maintaining the degree of progression required, deny her peers the chance to benefit from her presentation, and cause some inconvenience to the examiners who had joined the day's session. Considering these interests quickly, I replied, 'That is a shame, because you still have to do it today.' She looked surprised, went pale, swallowed hard and, after a few moments, said 'OK' in a tone that sounded anything but.

The session started as planned, and the participants made their presentations, including Bernie. Although it was clear that she was not well prepared, she made a good off-the-cuff presentation which delivered at least a good 'bluffer's guide' to her topic. Her peers, not knowing the background, took it at face value, and provided some accurate, constructive feedback.

Once the session was complete, Bernie and I had a few more moments together. I said that I was sorry she had found herself in a tight spot. She was gracious enough to say that, once the session had started, she could see why delay had not been an option. I smiled, and admitted that I had found it very hard to tell her that she had to do it. 'I felt like your Mum,' I said, 'telling you that you had to go to school when you didn't want to.' She grinned, and replied, 'No, you're not like my Mum – but it did feel like being in trouble back at school. But that was OK, because I liked that teacher too. I trusted him, and he didn't let me down.'

This type of incident is probably recognizable to all teachers. It is nonetheless interesting, as it illustrates a number of the issues we have been discussing.

First, it demonstrates the general nature of the teaching experience: whether working with an 11 year old, a mature student, or anyone else, all learners are likely to find themselves at odds with a situation from time to time, and they may face surprisingly similar difficulties which can generate feeling as well as uncovering those associated with the previous occasions upon which something similar happened.

Second, teachers become the focus of the teaching and learning process when they must exercise their professional judgement to weigh and balance the sometimes competing short-term and long-term interests of the individual learner, the interests of the learner's peers, the integrity of the learning process (including assessment) and the stability and maintenance of the learning environment (teaching staff, resources, etc.).

Third, the way in which I dealt with Bernie was important: I needed to take the time to give her my full attention, and to consider her request carefully. I needed to reach a conclusion as to the merits of her request, and to do so in the context of her immediate and longer-term needs, individually and as part of the group. She needed to see that I understood and acknowledged her concern, and that I reached my decision with that factor borne in mind. When I set her a challenge, she knew that I believed it was in her interests to attempt it, and that I believed she could meet it. We could both then have some confidence in my decision, even though it also aroused some trepidation on both sides. Considerations of confidence and trepidation also meant that I had to tailor my response in a certain way: at the very least, I needed to look confident and certain in my decision that Bernie would make her presentation regardless. In these particular circumstances, an appearance of doubt on my part (even if unintentionally while reaching my decision) would likely exacerbate her own anxious feelings, and thus impede her performance. This result would minimize the positive learning that she could take from the situation.

Fourth, the incident illustrates how individual character and past experience can have influences that one does not expect, even with learners with which the teacher is reasonably well acquainted. Bernie's comment about the influence of her school teacher is a classic example of transference. I had no reason to anticipate it, and yet it intervened to affect her response to the situation (in this instance, positively, encouraging her to trust my judgement). Similarly, even as a teacher with many years of experience, I had to exercise conscious control over my own feelings about the role I was playing, informed by my own experience as learner, peer and parent, as well as teacher.

Fifth, I had to make sure that my decision was based on relevant factors. As it happened, the session came immediately on the heels of a stressful morning: I was already slightly concerned by the need to ensure the afternoon ran smoothly in the light of the participants' needs, the presence of my three colleagues (who, ideally, should see the participants at their best in order to examine them to their potential, and, for the sake of my professional reputation, should ideally see me at my best) and the demands that the varying bits of technology requested by the participants would likely impose, even assuming that they would work at all. Acknowledging my own concerns but consciously placing my focus on Bernie permitted me to tune in to her interests, and those of the teaching and learning process.

Written in a very different (and more general) context to Salzberger-Wittenberg et al.'s (1999) reflective account of emotion in teaching and learning, Phillips' *On Kissing, Tickling and Being Bored* (1994) also presents a very good introduction to psychoanalytic perspectives. We can borrow the idea of 'tickling' for another insight into the role of social, environmental and emotional factors in teaching and learning.

Touch does not receive a great deal of attention in the mainstream literature on teaching and learning, except when dealing with it as a means to overcome visual disability. In the rare circumstances when it does – some colleagues, for example, recently completed a funded project to run an interdisciplinary network of academics, clinicians and museum professionals looking at object handling in a variety of contexts (see Chatterjee 2008; Pye 2007) – the focus tends to be on 'haptic' (i.e. touch-related) communication as a means of imparting data (regarding the nature of objects, for example).

I wrote about touch early in my career, exploring its role in learning and therapeutic contexts from a different perspective. It is well established that it is a vital sense for the newborn, both for data acquisition and in forming fundamental emotional bonds. Touch is often related to the profundities of human nature, including the formation of interpersonal trust (for which skin-to-skin contact may be very important) and even religion (the notion of 'healing hands', for example). Touch is also often a matter of taboo: its use is prescribed (and proscribed) by a range of subtle social cues (the complexity of which may vary significantly between cultures). At root of this sophistication is the recognition that touch may be an expression of power or control, quite apart from its practical, emotional, and other functions. In the UK, and in many other countries, public fear of interpersonal touch between adults and children (especially in the classroom) has arisen from the confusion of its purposes: in order to screen out instances of touch solely for the gratification of one party (particularly sexual touch which, in the adult–child context, becomes a deeply troubling expression of power; literally, an abuse), the notion of altruistic touch (which is not straight-forwardly an expression of power, but directed to emotional, practical and other functions) has also largely been eliminated from professional practice. This work is not a good forum to weigh the practical logic of this development against the deep roots associated with haptic communication, but it is worth highlighting that the use of some of the most fundamental human forms of expression (whether by physical touch or by engagement with an individual's emotional experience) may be as fraught with complications as it is effective. Indeed, precisely because of the range of subtleties that it approaches, I think touch is an excellent metaphor for teaching.

The discussion in the previous pages illustrates the way teaching is as much about relationships and human communities as it is about knowledge transfer. If we analyse the teaching and learning process in a transactional sense, it is clear that significant influences on the transaction stem from social, environmental and emotional factors. It is also important to recognize that teaching, although ostensibly directed solely to the fostering of learning, may also be an expression of power, affiliation and so on. For example (although we tend not to analyse it in these terms), the patronizing behaviour of a colleague can be interpreted as an unwarranted assumption of the teaching role. This interpersonal challenge (which may be conscious or unconscious) makes its recipient uncomfortable because it assumes the teacher's role (knowledgeable/powerful) while lacking the consensual foundation and legitimizing purpose of learning (quite apart from the professional ethical standards of the teacher). 'Non-formal' and 'informal' teaching and learning environments (see Chapter 6) may engender particular complexities in this regard, as the teacher's role may be more or less well defined.

Teaching is also culturally embedded. In the same way that the socially acceptable use of touch requires great cultural awareness, so does the teacher's legitimate professional attempt to optimize the learning relationship. Teachers must always be alert to the possibilities of cultural misunderstanding, which may lead (at the very least) to impeded learning if not outright alienation.

The example perhaps most relevant to the present day is the tension caused by the choice of some learners (and/or teachers) to adopt the *hijab*. (Literally meaning 'cover' in Arabic, the term *hijab* is used rather loosely in the media to include various forms of Islamic dress which tend to obscure the face.) The teacher is, of course, professionally obliged to respect the personal choices, moral values, and religious beliefs of the learner. Although the teaching curriculum may, in certain circumstances, permit or encourage challenge to some or all the participants' values, this may only be done consensually, in a fundamentally supportive and thoughtful way, and when all participants (teacher(s) and learner(s)) are suitably prepared for the experience. From these basic principles, it would seem that the teacher must respect the expression of the learner's religious beliefs (or vice versa) through the wearing of the *hijab*.

At the same time, this chapter has stressed the importance of face-to-face engagement as a core part of the teaching and learning process: does the use of the *hijab* necessarily compromise the teacher's professionalism? We can answer this question with a qualified 'no'. The teacher should be aware that the *hijab* may well have a significant effect on the teaching and learning process – but this should definitely not lead them to an inflexible, knee-jerk reaction. At the same time, the clear obligation (socially, professionally and as a matter of institutional policy) to respect and promote a diverse society does not translate into a prohibition on any action at all. The teacher should take steps in partnership with the learner(s) to confirm their understanding of the relevant etiquette, and explore ways in which communication may be acceptably optimized. The teacher should also consider the impact that an individual's use of the *hijab* may have on other members of the class. Will the teacher inadvertently pay more attention to uncovered learners than those who are covered? Conversely, will the teacher overcompensate, and sideline the rest of the class in the interest of promoting maximum engagement with the *hijab*-wearing learner? Will the group of the learners in the minority feel isolated? Will the group of learners in the majority feel excluded? The range of questions which the teacher may need to consider (and potentially take action upon) may be great indeed, depending on the particular issue which has arisen.

It should be emphasized that, although the *hijab* is a contemporary preference to which teachers should give some thought, there is a vast range of other cultural preferences (let alone merely individual characteristics) which may affect the teaching and learning process. (In the context of higher education in London, one of the biggest 'cultural' clashes between teachers and learners revolves (surprisingly) around food: I have talked to no end of teachers who have been completely blind-sided by their difficulty in achieving a 'meeting of minds' with learners who see no issue arising from consuming (hot!) food in the middle of class.) The teacher should pursue the same basic process in all cases – although, depending on the degree to which the apparent cultural or individual attribute clearly represents a deliberate attempt to get away with antisocial behaviour (which may have been the case for some of the mid-class nibblers), a slightly more muscular response may be appropriate.

Above all, one of the teacher's core professional obligations is the *duty to pay attention* to the various circumstances which may influence the teaching and learning process, to consider their impact, and to take active steps to promote or mitigate them as required. Although this chapter emphasizes the value of face-to-face communication, this should not be taken as an absolute injunction. Rather, this form of communication is usually the optimal, when all other factors are equal. In instances when other factors prevent the optimal solution (and these will be many and varied), the teacher's duty is to find creative solutions to maximize the relationship within the framework of the resources (personal, physical, environmental, etc.) that they have at their disposal. A teacher of professional mastery is able to improvise effectively in the exercise of their function.

If, as I suggest, we can use touch as a useful metaphor for teaching in general, I also offer tickling as an apt analogy for a particular instance of teaching which rarely receives sufficient consideration.

To be effective, tickling depends on a very particular mix of spontaneity, intimacy and helplessness. It is not a form of expression generally appropriate between strangers, and, even when attempted in such a context, is unlikely to meet with success. Tickling creates a particular (if transitory) bond: the parties involved permit themselves to become vulnerable to one another – and trust that they know when to stop, both for themselves and the other. Tickling frequently leads to a reversal of roles, the tickl*er* becomes the tickl*ee*, and back again; power is distributed between both parties.

A certain experience of teaching, which has no formal name of which I am aware, although it has a certain resemblance to aspects of the 'flow' state (see Chapter 6), is analogous to tickling. It is not strictly a method of teaching in its own right as it can take place instead within the context of any teaching approach (although it is more likely to happen in the context of methods which promote greater interaction between teacher and learner(s)). Just like tickling, it is characterized by a strong bond of trust between teacher and learner(s), which develops spontaneously in the course of sustained activity, and which serves to level the playing field, opening the teacher up to the possibility of learning from their students, even as the reverse is true. At its essence, this experience of teaching is the joyous part, the moment at which it is the purest fun, a peak experience – for teachers, as well as for learners. It cannot be easily evaluated, or reproduced on demand; it arises and develops in a way that is meaningful for those involved, but may not be readily comprehensible to others. It can be a very powerful learning experience; it may account for many of the specific incidents which learners recall when asked to identify 'favourite' teachers. To a great extent, the feelings engendered may themselves represent a significant part of the learning experience, shaping future patterns of interest and behaviour.

There is no doubt that this experience of teaching and learning is one of the defining moments of education. Representations of the educational experience in the popular media frequently depict scenarios of this sort as its apogee (the early experiences of John Keating's class in the film *The Dead Poets' Society* (1989) present one good example). Teachers must exercise great caution, however, when they feel themselves begin to 'enter the zone' in this way. They must always be alert to the possibility that, although this experience of teaching and learning is often very inclusive, it is not inevitably so. They must be careful to avoid a sensation of exclusion for those who 'don't get it', and work to help them.

Closely related to the idea of tickling is the idea of humour in teaching and learning. Humour can be used in a wide variety of contexts, and often represents an effective way to augment the teaching and learning experience. Much of our developmental trajectory (at least for those brought up in western cultures) encourages adults to put aside childish frivolity and assume the seriousness of purpose which is deemed to be a characteristic of adulthood. Play and work are to be clearly distinguished and, for many, there is little daily experience of joy in their work. We have a chance to frame learning differently, however, so that it can be a joyful experience.

Expert teachers are in control of the humour of a class. They do not seek always to be the source of amusement – indeed, it is much better when a group is blessed by learners who will share responsibility for this vital function – but it is the teacher who creates the climate within which such shared responsibility can flourish. Jokes can sometimes be used to illustrate difficult points with an eloquence that more sober forms of language rarely achieve (see Cathcart and Klein 2007). In this context, they also represent an original and elegant form of self-assessment: getting the joke can also show that the learner 'gets' the concept. Teachers who take jokes in the right way gain considerable status with most groups. Shared jokes help to establish a group identity. They can release tension, burst the bubble of pomposity, build confidence, invert the normal power relationships and express warmth. In short, learning is at its most effective when it is fun – and this is not incompatible with it being serious, purposeful and challenging.

It should be noted, however, that humour is personal and inherently risky. Most of us will occasionally come across a joke that we find embarrassing or in poor taste. Use of humour must, therefore, be appropriate to the context; pejorative jokes will not be so, except in the rarest of circumstances. Humour will sometimes strike learners as genuinely funny; more often it will serve to put them at ease, ensuring they have sufficient emotional energy to tackle the challenge of learning. Having fun in learning does not just have to be about being *fun-ny*. There are so many other ways that a serious atmosphere can also be light-hearted. Whatever you do, it has to work for you. Learners catch enthusiasm for your topic. They know if you would really rather be doing something else. Even the topic or activities which we find it hard to enjoy need to be approached as if they are intrinsically entertaining.

Conclusion

Promoting wellbeing within education, for both teacher and learner, depends primarily on recognizing that participants are complex, diverse individuals with varying physical, emotional and cognitive needs and preferences. They arrive at the learning event as adults, influenced (even defined) by rich personal histories and prior educational experience. These experiences may interact with the teaching and learning process in unpredictable ways. Teachers cannot anticipate all the ways in which the myriad factors which define learners as individuals will play out in the classroom. They can, however, create a positive, safe climate of respect and trust. This is good for learning anyway, and makes it much easier to deal with the unexpected legacies of adult life, as and when they arise.

This chapter is long on principles, and short on practical tips. This is hardly surprising; people do not act or react 'by numbers'. However, to achieve a climate likely to support learning, teachers might like to consider the following techniques. It should be readily noticeable that they all depend upon, or fall within, the vitally important process of attending to the learners. Teaching is not just about output; it is just as important to listen, to watch and to think.

- Contain learners' emotions when they cannot do so themselves.
- Attend to learners' needs, not just their desires.
- Keep learners informed about their learning; wherever practical, consult them.
- Recognize when an individual learner is like everyone else, someone else and nobody else – and then treat them appropriately.
- Listen.
- Watch.
- Value one's own expertise and share it generously.
- Be steadfast when the going gets tough.
- Share the learners' joy in discovery, lessons learned, trials overcome.

- Be amusing (but try to avoid being facile).
- Try to be worthy of the learners' attention (while not dependent upon universal admiration).
- Notice if learners are unhappy, discouraged or in jeopardy.
- Notice if learners are joyful, content or having a good time.
- Trust learners' ability to persevere – think about when an intervention is required, and when learners will benefit from rising to challenges themselves.
- Attend, unfailingly, to the details of politeness, hospitality, kindness and generosity that one would expect on arrival at a welcoming home.

There are also some surprisingly straightforward steps that teachers can take to promote a positive disposition towards themselves. Some key ones have been set out below; readers are likely to come up with their own too. Many of these steps are about presentation: if you can manage to present yourself simultaneously as not only a real person, but also a teacher, it is remarkable how much will follow. Difficulties in managing relationships with learners may often stem from an imbalance in presenting these two facets.

Before starting

- Try to be the first one in the room – about five minutes ahead of the learners is perfect. This shows respect, allows you time to collect yourself, and grants the opportunity to pay attention to the learners as they arrive.
- If you cannot arrive before the learners, plan your entrance. Be like an actor: make sure you project an image that will enhance the teaching and learning process.
- Smile! Look pleased to be teaching, and in the company of your learners.
- Talk! If there is an opportunity for natural conversation with one or more individuals, take it. If the opportunity does not present itself, do not strive officiously for it.
- Welcome people to the session – individually, if the group is small, or otherwise broken down in the best way you can.
- At your first session, greet and make the acquaintance of learners as you would anyone else (at least as far as reasonably practicable). If you would shake their hand when meeting socially or for business, then do so. Adult learners are real people. Treat them like it.

With large groups

- Work the audience, especially before starting. Engage them (with energy!) in simple question and response ('Is there anyone in from Blackpool?', etc.); get them used to your pitch and manner of delivery, and you to theirs. I have not yet had to resort to cards marked 'Laugh', 'Applaud' or 'Cheer' but you never know, it may happen one day . . .
- When speaking to a large audience (assuming you can see them), find someone a few rows from the back who is willing to make eye contact (and maybe even give you a smile): *begin* by addressing your remarks to this person. This will give you some confidence if you find large numbers a bit intimidating.
- Otherwise, make sure you keep your head up, and your delivery measured. If you can comfortably avoid referring to written material, do so. If using a lectern, do not cling to it! Relax – and maybe even venture out from behind it.
- If reading some or all of a presentation to a large audience, use a lectern and consider (discreetly!) following your place with a finger (like you may have done as a kid). This enables you to look up at important moments and not be worried you will lose your place. This, of course, works only if you have a 'friendly' lectern or reading desk. You do not want the audience to see you are doing it.
- Look at your learners. Watch their expressions. Try to talk to them, rather than delivering at them. With practice, you will get good at reading expressions and gaining feedback: trust it. If they look flustered, slow down; it they look confused, repeat or rephrase the point; if they look bored, take a moment to disturb the routine.
- Vary your gaze. Try not to fixate on one or two members of the group listening; it can make them surprisingly uncomfortable.
- Be upbeat, audible and energetic for at least a proportion of the time. You may also want to encourage times of quietness, reflection and introverted space as well.

With groups of any size

- Consider how different live performers work an audience. Do they have anything to offer you?
- Think carefully about anecdotes – consider what they are intended to illustrate. Do not get into them unless you know precisely how you are going to get out of them. Don't ramble.

- Change the learning activity every 15–20 minutes.
- In appropriate circumstances, include 'games' as an opportunity for interactivity and amusement. Make sure you find a convenient role for yourself when this occurs, moderating or participating. Do not get stuck waiting awkwardly for them to finish.
- Encourage universal (or near as you can get) contribution from learners. Make use of available resources (electronic student response technology, self-adhesive notes, flags, 'voting cards', arm waving, or calling out).
- Use props, toys and pictures to surprise and engage.
- Tease learners you know – if you are *sure* you will not humiliate or embarrass.
- Being teased is good too. Accept it as an expression of trust and affection.
- Do not hide behind your technology – MS Powerpoint can be great or it can be very boring. Sometimes, it is good to *plan* a session with Powerpoint but then *present* it without.
- If you are in a diverse environment (ethnicity, gender, age, background), guard against bias in your selection of examples, anecdotes or illustrations.
- If you are unsure whether something will offend, check! (For example, I normally provide refreshments for the start of modules I teach; one year my teaching began in Ramadan. I checked with learners to make sure that offering food did not cause difficulties, or serve to exclude anyone. It demonstrated that I was preparing for them as people and that their wellbeing, as individuals, mattered to me.)
- Be kind.
- Be human. You are allowed to feel things: although you should retain a degree of self-control, let the learners know when you are pleased – and occasionally when you are not.
- When in doubt, a bit of exaggeration, self-caricature, self-parody or disarming honesty is often useful. Don't overdo it.
- Encourage playfulness, creativity and spontaneity. Through giving clear signals, help learns to know when such behaviour is appropriate.
- Where numbers and practicalities permit, get to know your learners – especially names and basic backgrounds.
- Be clear about boundaries: you are a real person but you are *their teacher* for the duration of your professional relationship.
- Think about how much of yourself you wish to reveal in your teaching: some personal examples may be excellent in the right situation but, in other contexts, more formality may be necessary.

Match your approach to the context. (For example, among MA students I use personal illustrations; when working in a prison I do not reveal any personal information.)
- Vary your vocal tone, pitch and volume.
- Seek advice and peer feedback on *how* you teach, not just what you teach.
- Get professional guidance about improving your teaching techniques.
- Get the learners to share the task of presenting in a range of ways (formal and informal; prepared and spontaneous; alone or in groups; in verse or song).

6 Learning outside the classroom: Informal and non-formal learning, motivation and flow

This chapter explores the teaching and learning which take place outside the context of institutions dedicated solely to the purpose. The wider world of teaching and learning is great indeed, ranging from professional development to the pursuit of personal 'hobbies', and including those forms of learning which occur when the situation prompts them, just for their own sake. The teacher's role, status and function in these contexts are much less well defined than in the formal sphere, and require some clarification. Despite appearances, we can declare that teachers are by no means confined to classrooms, nor are they irrelevant to the wide range of environments in which modern learning is expected to take place.

For those interested in adult learning and professional development, the transition from the twentieth to the twenty-first century has been distinguished by two big ideas, which have encouraged a much broader conception of the role and significance of learning. Paradoxically, these ideas have led to a contemporary tendency to sideline the teacher from many learning scenarios. This tendency is wrong.

The first big idea was that every adult is personally responsible for their own learning. Each of us must continue to learn in order to equip ourselves for the changing demands of the labour market and to keep up with the wider requirements of contemporary society. We may need to refresh our acquaintance with the latest technological innovation and/or adapt to new organizational systems and practices while at work (such as health and safety, quality assurance, data protection and freedom of information). Outside working hours, twenty-first-century adults living in the developed world also participate in learning activities through the need to engage in appropriate physical exercise and the need to fulfil citizenship duties (including financial planning, informed contributions to civil decision-making, ethical action upon environmental issues, care for dependent relatives, and 'neighbourliness'). Adults may also choose to participate in artistic, cultural and recreational activities which contribute to quality of life and mental/spiritual wellbeing, and which often contain a significant learning component. Although many of these demands on our time are not new, it is true to say that there seem to be many more of them. Moreover, whereas these activities may once have been dismissed (perhaps foolishly) as mere hobbies, they are now increasingly seen as different manifestations of a common ideal: learning as a life-wide, as well as lifelong, activity. Quite apart from the individual benefits that these activities confer, they also have a significant social return, contributing to a more integrated, fitter, and more intellectually and economically competitive population.

The recent political attention given to the ageing population in Europe, and the wider economic impact that this trend will have, has given an additional fillip to the notion of personal responsibility for lifelong learning. Older people may need to remain economically active for longer, and so retraining could become an economic imperative. Alternatively, as the first 'mass leisure class in history' (Anderson 1999: 90), retired older people may seek (and may require) various other forms of learning along the lines articulated earlier in order to enhance or maintain their quality of life. Inter-generational learning, perhaps itself as old as the hills, has seen a recent surge of interest in Europe (see, e.g. the ADD LIFE European Tool Kit; Waxenegger 2008).

The second big idea was that a lot – indeed, perhaps, most – of the modern panoply of learning will take place outside the context of full-time study in traditional educational institutions (schools, colleges, universities). This second idea is primarily a logical extension of the first. If adults bear the responsibility for continuing learning and professional development throughout their lives, it must be accessible in forms compatible with the myriad commitments that compete for a normal adult's attention. This means learning opportunities must be available through work, through leisure, and indeed incidentally to almost any other activity. In practical terms, this means that a vast number of adults assume a degree of responsibility for the learning of others merely by meeting their own daily commitments – and as the general imperative to learn is made more overt, so is the teaching role of those who find themselves assisting in the process. In this context, teaching has become a much more common task, and there is the potential for its substantial weakening as a discrete professional identity. How do we begin to recognize, assist and develop the increasing numbers of people who (through choice or circumstance) have assumed responsibility for the learning of others?

The increased 'push' of IT-based learning solutions by public and private sector organizations, intended for individuals to access independently, is one response to the perceived increase in learning needs and the practical limitations that seem to exist in teaching support. It is not necessarily the simple solution that it seems, however (nor the threat to the professional domain of the teacher): there are developing indications that such methods may make learners feel rather lonely and unsupported, a particular difficulty when professional and personal isolation may be a growing problem for mid-life and older adults. As already discussed (see Chapter 2), online learning tools seem to be most effective when used in conjunction with teaching support remote or face to face, rather than independently of it.

What, then, is the role of the teacher in this new model of life-wide learning? Are teachers absent or merely hidden? Are they fit for purpose? Do our traditional notions of what it means to be a professional teacher fit in with conceptions of the teacher required by contemporary circumstances? This chapter explores these questions while also celebrating the pleasure of learning as it occurs in unexpected corners of sometimes over-busy lives. In so doing, it focuses attention on notions of teaching as a catalyst for the process of learning, wherever it takes place.

Informal and non-formal contexts for learning

In 2000 the European Commission published a memorandum on life-long learning, which defined three contexts within which learning takes place: formal, non-formal and informal. Roughly, these translate into the real world in the following way:

- *Formal* learning environments – public or private institutions primarily dedicated to learning, most of which is formally accredited, for example universities, colleges and schools.
- *Non-formal* learning environments – public or private institutions where learning is intended to take place but as a secondary priority for the organization. Learning may be accredited, usually by a third party (for example, National Council for Vocational Qualifications or a formal learning partner); for example museums, galleries, hospitals, businesses, churches and other faith communities.
- *Informal* learning environments – any context (which may or may not be institutional) in which learning takes place incidental to another activity, and normally unforeseen and unplanned, for example childrearing, care of elderly people, political activism, worship, social involvement in the arts.

It should be apparent from these examples that an exploration of learning and teaching outside the classroom is an exploration of the non-formal and informal contexts of learning and teaching. For convenience here, these are collectively termed informal/non-formal contexts. The work of teachers in these contexts has received less critical attention and practical exposition within the literature than that of their colleagues in formal educational contexts. This chapter begins to redress that balance. This work deserves consideration for five reasons.

Growing significance in social policy

Informal/non-formal learning contexts have acquired greater significance in the social policy arena in recent years. Greater understanding of the processes of learning and teaching outside conventional 'classrooms' has become a priority as public authorities seek to conscript untapped potential to meet new social, political and economic challenges. These contexts should be more widely acknowledged and understood if they are to be properly resourced to deliver the outcomes anticipated.

Claims made about positive learning outcomes derived from informal/non-formal contexts, translating into socially 'useful' people, are frequently anecdotal and partisan, often made by enthusiastic practitioners or satisfied customers in highly particular situations. Where such claims have any empirical basis, they are frequently based only upon small samples, such as pilot studies. There is, however, early evidence that 'wellbeing' (an identified set of physical, emotional and cognitive indicators) among adults – and particularly within the important older age groups – is positively influenced by engagement in learning activities (Pye 2007; Schuller et al. 2004). Stronger research evidence will be required if policy decisions leading towards the allocation of more substantial and increasingly scarce resources are to be made for the maximum public good.

Demand for recognition of life experience in formal study

There is a growing demand among adult learners for the recognition and consolidation of life-wide learning experiences in the formal learning context.

With increasing frequency, adults taking up or returning to formal study seek the recognition of credit acquired in prior formal learning (a process sometimes known as the Accreditation of Prior Learning: APL) and/or exemption from certain aspects of academic or vocational programmes on the basis of previously unaccredited knowledge acquired in the course of their daily lives (also known as the Accreditation of Prior Experiential Learning: APEL). These processes are more complex and technically challenging than may be first realized. To preserve the integrity of the course upon which the learner has enrolled, the learner's APL/APEL request must be supported by evidence presented in a way which enables an appropriate comparison and standardization to be made, an often difficult and frustrating task. Formal learning institutions cannot fail to impose such requirements for fear of devaluing their own 'brands'. At the same time, they may come under increasing pressure to develop APL/APEL systems to meet this demand.

At best, an APL/APEL application can represent a good learning exercise for the individual concerned: in making their case, they revisit and reconsider their original learning, often to their benefit. At worst, the process may be more problematic than simply taking the course for which the exemption is sought. The process can also be quite emotionally charged; many learners feel (rightly or wrongly) that it represents an evaluation of their personal worth, professional expertise or good standing. From the institution's side, the process requires an individual with a sound professional background in teaching and learning, in order to be able to interpret the learner's information fully and properly (which may not always be presented in the optimum manner).

A better understanding of the teaching and learning process as it takes place in informal/non-formal contexts, and the resonance with professional practice in formal institutions, can thus only facilitate APL/APEL requests in the future, and augment the service formal education institutions can offer to differently experienced adult learners.

The benefit of shared good practice

Whenever possible, all professional groups benefit from shared good practice. Teaching is no different. The diversity of learning environments means that practitioners from formal and informal/non-formal learning contexts are likely to have gained different insights into the practice of supporting and enhancing learning. Sharing this information is in the interest of professional teaching as a whole. Practitioners need evidence of what works for their peers, a grasp of the possible explanations about why it works that way, and an idea of what to do if it does not work. Denying information from one source or the other makes little sense. Further, teachers (and learners) may gain specific insights from greater awareness of the impact of the learning environment (and the learner's role within it) that experience derived from a different learning context will provide.

Opportunities for innovation and expertise transfer

Informal/non-formal learning contexts provide opportunities for innovation in teaching and learning that may not be otherwise available. They raise interesting (and sometimes unique) questions about what people tend to learn and/or value in a given situation, as well as the way in which learning occurs. Teaching experience in these contexts, provoking and enabling teachers to experiment with non-traditional approaches and new technologies, has positively influenced practice in formal circumstances. This practice may then be mainstreamed and developed within the new context.

Experience gained in one context may be communicated to practitioners working in the other, or may be exported more directly. Teachers experienced in informal/non-formal learning contexts may choose to migrate into schools, colleges and universities. Similarly, teachers trained and experienced in work in formal learning environments may also progress the other way, finding useful and stimulating roles in a range of situations, including museums and galleries, hospitals, media and public relations outlets, charities, politics, churches, community development initiatives and so on. This circulation of talent is beneficial not only to the enhanced professionalism of teachers and teaching, but also to the wider social objective in promoting a learning society.

Professional careers for teachers in the future can be more widely conceived, and planned progression between all three learning contexts is likely to raise standards, encourage cross-fertilization and retain talent within the sphere of teaching. School teaching, for example, has a relatively high rate of attrition: this represents a loss of 'vocational capital'. It may well be that experienced teachers might plan to move from the classroom into a wide range of other environments in which learning potential (and the opportunity for teachers) is not yet fully realized.

Conceptual problems and ambiguities require solving

Finally, informal/non-formal learning contexts form an interesting and worthwhile subject for study in their own right. Even the conclusion that the four reasons already outlined are not persuasive illustrates that we do not understand the processes involved in 'outside' learning sufficiently. Research in this area is not easy, not least because the distinction between non-formal contexts and informal contexts is less clear cut than it may appear. Scoping research with sufficient accuracy to produce meaningful conclusions is a challenge. Even then, the outcome is likely to be situationally specific, depend on qualitative rather than quantitative research methods, be vulnerable to conflicting analyses, and generate few straight answers. Ethnographic approaches (in which researchers inhabit particular communities in order to understand them) and even autoethnography (in which the researcher reports systematically on their own experience) may be helpful. I have personally found this technique helpful in exploring certain issues in this field.

For the present purposes, however, we can accept that informal/non-formal learning contexts are likely to make a significant contribution to the lifelong learning agenda, and that this will be felt both inside and outside formal education institutions. It must be asked then whether absolutely anywhere can be a context for learning, or whether there is an essential quality or resource which determines an environment's educational potential.

Realizing informal and non-formal teaching and learning contexts

One analysis of learning regards it as the adaptation of behaviour in the light of experience. On this basis, any experience results in learning. Common sense, however, tells us that it is not quite that simple. Many of us will know people who have had several years' experience of a particular activity, but behave as if they had the benefit of only a short period. Rather than adapting to changing circumstances, and drawing on a wider span of experience, they have become stuck in a narrow range which they effectively repeat multiple times. It is more accurate to conclude, therefore, that any situation may represent a *potential* learning environment. The 2008 advertising campaign for the English Learning and Skills Council asserts (rather loosely) that humans are 'genetically programmed' to learn. There is a kernel of truth in the idea of this learning disposition, but the conditions in which the potential of a learning environment is realized are more complex.

A full account of the factors which mark the transition from a potential learning environment to a realized learning environment would take a whole book, and require an engagement with the philosophical and psychological implications of the idea of 'learning' that would occupy many more. However, one simple answer, applicable in a range of circumstances, is that the existence of a teacher significantly enhances the potential of any context to result in learning. The proponents of andragogy and social constructivism (as models of learning) highlight the importance of opportunities to build on and adapt existing knowledge and experience through interaction with peers. The management of this process may be difficult, however, and especially so in less formal contexts. Experience and expertise may not be distributed equally through the community, and their distribution may not correlate with personal preferences in the management of the discussion. I believe that the role of teacher, broadly defined, is rarely left open in these circumstances. We all benefit if this process becomes explicit, transparent and responsibility for it appropriately shared.

In formal (and some non-formal) learning contexts, we might consider that the teacher has 'ascribed' status: their presence and identity is easily recognizable by virtue of their 'publicity'. As learners, we tend to recognize teachers as 'teachers' not because of their particular merit (although we are pleased when we see some sign of this) but because of the name plate on their door, their job title, their physical presentation to us, and so on. However, in most informal/non-formal learning contexts, the teacher may lack this ascribed status. We may learn things from people but this appears to happen on a more ad-hoc basis. In these circumstances, it is more apt to describe individuals as possessing 'achieved' status, occupying the role of teacher on the basis of accepted personal ability and merit. Whereas ascribed status requires a social consensus about the identity of the teacher (i.e. the institution must recognize an individual as a teacher, a decision to which learners are then expected to defer), achieved status requires a negotiated consensus between peers (i.e. not only must the candidate teacher think that they possess relevant ability but also any and all candidate learners must accept this proposition).

Informal/non-formal teaching and learning contexts *may* be more likely to be realized, therefore, when an individual achieves 'teacherly' status in a potential learning environment. The role that these individuals play, and the extent to which their practice is consistent with the professional character of teachers in more formal contexts, remains quite opaque.

There are clearly occasions, however, when society does not wish learning potential to be realized (or, at least, not in a particular form), and certainly where it is inappropriate for the label of 'teacher' to be applied. Personal experience of work within English prisons has led me to reflect upon the difficulty of ensuring that the prison population learns 'positively' rather than 'negatively' from their time inside. There is little doubt that, when left to their own devices, many adults will in fact learn those attitudes, behaviours and skills which come most easily, rather than those which are more socially desirable. Various individuals in this context may achieve a 'teacherly' role. In considering the breadth of possible learning environments, therefore, we are forced to make a distinction (which is almost inescapably subjective, and based on political/social/ moral values) about what constitutes 'useful' learning. This process, which may be uncomfortable, informs the question of the role of 'teachers', who may serve two purposes. First, they may, in certain circumstances, alter the balance between 'positive' and 'negative' learning, influencing adults to learn in a socially desired fashion. Second, and perhaps even more importantly, teachers drastically increase the probability of sustainable learning taking place, and enhancing its outcome. A teacher's expertise may also help to spin off learning in unanticipated directions, useful to the learner. Teaching contributes to increasing the likelihood that the learning potential of a situation will be realized by at least some actual learners. To do this spontaneous or random behaviours within a particular context might be directed, enhanced and sustained until they have borne sufficient fruit for the learner to assume personal responsibility for their continuation. The learning from informal/non-formal environments is often recognizably different from that supported by formal contexts in that when the teacher withdraws from the context, the learning will often continue. Formal learning in educational institutions tends to stop or be put on hold if teaching input is interrupted. During the second half of this chapter we shall look further at some of the conditions which might characterize the contexts for informal/non-formal learning.

Working with the environment and seizing opportunities

Learning which takes place in informal/non-formal contexts generally also happens within physical environments which are not primarily designed for the purpose of learning. The hospital ward is constructed and organized to care for the sick; the river is what topography and recent weather determine will become the path of water towards the sea; the gallery is intended to collect, conserve, interpret and display art objects. Learning can occur (clinical diagnosis, canoeing or art appreciation and history respectively) in or on each of them but it is incidental to their primary functions. Teaching in such contexts requires adaptation to working with what is available, rather than specifying precise requirements and conditions. Assistance in interaction with the environment is, in fact, one of the chief functions of the teacher in informal/non-formal learning. Let us consider briefly the way teachers direct, enhance and sustain learning to illustrate the process of working in these contexts.

Direction includes ensuring that learners attend to the most relevant aspects of the particular environment and perform appropriate tasks within it. This may require focus on the most important and/or accessible details at first, paying particular attention to any matters of health and safety. Then in a timely and coherent way, attention is focused on those aspects of the environment which yield information which is transformed by the learner into knowledge, understanding and skill. In an informal learning environment there may be nobody or several people undertaking some aspects of this function, on some occasions rather than all of the time. Sometimes it is when an individual indicates a need for help that they will receive it from any one or more of a number of possible sources. Direction can be aimed at the realization of the learning potential of the situation (in which case someone has adopted the role of teacher) or it can distract and inhibit the learning.

Enhancement will almost certainly include the introduction of some technical terms which aid precision in the use of language and facilitate common labelling of the same items by all participants in the particular learning discourse. (You can have some fun trying to teach your own area of expertise without using any 'technical' language – it gets very difficult to do.) Clinicians, canoeists and art historians belong to communities of practice or disciplines or professions. Whatever collective noun we use (and they are all open to debate), it does not make sense for learners to claim that they have learned any one of these activities but have nothing in common with other people who have also learned them. So it is likely that teachers enhance the process of individual experimentation which is possible in clinical diagnosis (although, one hopes, in a fairly restricted fashion!), canoeing and art history by inducting learners into ways of describing and/or demonstrating what they can do in language and/or actions which are recognized by their more experienced colleagues. In other words, teaching in this context can be performed by any more experienced inhabitant of the learning environment. It will vary qualitatively (or take a particular disciplinary focus) depending on the experience, background and resolution of the person who is engaging in the conversation with the novice learner.

Finally, sustaining learning is the process by which the teacher, through feedback (both motivational and evaluative), ensures that a participant persists with the learning long enough, and in the most productive way, for learning to have time to occur. For example, I once spent a long time failing to teach myself to 'eskimo roll' a canoe. As I was about to give up, from tiredness and disappointment, a friend described the technique, demonstrated it in her own boat and then got into the water so that she could grab my hand at the right moment to pull me above the surface to complete the roll. She had been enjoying her own paddling when she noticed that I had most of the technique but was tiring and just failing to make the final flick into the upright position. The pleasure triggered by the experience of success with her help motivated me to go on practising for much longer until I had achieved my goal. It cost my friend some time standing up to her waist in cold water, but she could not resist helping me. Her intervention realized the potential of the learning environment. She had no formal duty to teach me, and I did not have to accept her help. Teaching in the informal/non-formal contexts is more likely to occur through sharing as situations present themselves, than as a result of detailed planning. Those who would teach in such places have to be alert for the moments when people are ready to learn without expecting them to have made a prior commitment to a full course of lessons.

Visiting Tate Modern: why look at art when you can spend more time in the café?

There is something satisfying about being outside the system and learning something your own way. As we have already seen, this does not mean it is all done alone, just that the people who assist us may not be obliged to do so, or they may not be there the next time we enter the place where we first learned from them. We exist together in the kind of purity of mutual interdependence bound only, if at all, by a common interest and/or a personal relationship.

You may, now, be thinking that this is all very well, but how does it help advance the effectiveness, recognition and status of learning gained through informal/non-formal contexts? Furthermore, how does it help teachers enable learners to be ready and able to become self-directing and purposeful when they experience a potential learning environment without any of the normal educational systems or incentives to progress? I hope you were asking yourself such things, as these were the kinds of question that a unique afternoon at an art gallery in 2002 prompted me to ask of myself.

I made some notes of that particular visit to the Tate. They provide a record of the event from my point of view at the time. The detail is selective and my interpretation was limited, but a few weeks after the visit I returned to them and the memory of the visit prompted me to further action. So I spent an afternoon at the British Library searching the catalogue for literature which might contribute to an interpretation of the personal event in a wider context. I was surprised to find striking similarities between my account and those reported as given by others in similar circumstances. Many of the attributes of that day seem to chime with descriptions of the way other adults felt when surprised by powerful learning in an unexpected place. Although I had visited galleries before, I was not prepared for what was to happen that day. My journal records the events as follows.

> We looked at a picture by Henri Matisse (*The Moroccans*: see Cowling et al. 2002) for much, much longer than I would normally have done. The work was large, striking and composed of brightly coloured geometric shapes. Claire [my companion and guide for the visit] asked what I thought it was. This question was significantly different from her previous ones. It required me to make a judgement rather than simply describe what I could see or thought I liked.

Until this point, there had been no possibility that my answers might be wrong. Now my ignorance could be exposed. What if my interpretation of this complex image was ludicrous? I struggled to find a way in and to think of something to say. Eventually, I replied that the lower left-hand corner looked like watermelons on a checked table-cloth. She paused before observing that they were generally interpreted as turbaned figures kneeling in prayer! I was much amused by this ambiguity, while being acutely aware that under different circumstances such situations had caused me to feel foolish and resentful. Humour and the pain of humiliation often coexist in tension when you are learning. The presence or absence of trust tends to determine which will prevail. The consequences of that particular moment feel enormous. The thing was . . . it felt safe . . . yet risky at the same time. I loved it.

(Personal journal entry)

When challenged to say what I could see in Matisse's painting, I experienced what has been described as a 'crystallizing experience' (Walters and Gardner 1986, cited by Csikszentmihalyi and Hermanson 1999: 146). This vivid expression seems apt for the moment when an event which might previously have had only marginal and short-lived significance is recognized as having the potential to sustain an enduring engagement with similar events. It left me with a powerful motivation to understand what had happened. Such drive towards understanding was fuelled by a personal desire to be able to enjoy looking at art in this way again and to discover what other information had contributed to the orthodox interpretation of the Matisse picture. It also reflected a rather cooler professional interest as a teacher. I wanted to be able to do what Claire instinctively did for me. I wanted to understand how to unlock the learning potential of diverse environments. This is no easy task. I have not got all the answers here, but sustained enquiry into this topic has led me towards some tentative conclusions. I am developing my own practice around a combination of ideas arising from an exploration of four elements:

- Individual differences in cognitive functioning
- Confronting dilemmas which prompt a reappraisal of current assumptions
- Learning as a socio-cultural practice
- Pleasure and the motivation towards sustaining it.

As we look at each of these in turn you will recognize that I have already introduced some of the basic ideas in earlier chapters. Taken together they provide some clues for developing practice within informal/ non-formal contexts.

Jung's theories about the human personality led to the development of a typology for working with individual differences in cognitive functioning. I introduced some of the basic information about this in Chapter 4. There, it is used to raise awareness of the impact that individual differences may have on assessment. In this chapter, it may assist us to consider how different people tend to behave in complex, multi-sensory environments, like art galleries or museums.

When people look at art (particularly in a busy gallery) many stimuli compete for attention and tiny decisions are made without most people even being aware of making them. My experience at the Tate made me wonder about the way individuals actually organize their attention within the exhibition space. Museums and galleries enable all psychological types to organize a visit in ways which suit them as individuals. They will of course also be responding to more or less subtle expressions of the preferences and/or professional intentions of curators and designers of the exhibition itself. For some visitors, the preferred way of absorbing information and making decisions about it will be chosen very consistently. Such people may also have a very strong sense of there being a 'right way' to approach any similar situation. They may be highly selective in paying attention. They may gain substantially from exposure to a limited range of already valued material but may find themselves very disorientated if confronted by unexpected or differently presented stimuli. People with different psychological preferences may tend towards greater mental flexibility. Those who have learned to feel comfortable with all the cognitive functions in both attitudes may be more adaptable in their response to the opportunities available in a particular situation, but they may also be overwhelmed by too many choices in a very rich and possibly unfamiliar environment.

Psychological type theory suggests some clues about the way different people may be organizing their cognitive resources while visiting a gallery or museum. Since the attitudes and functions combine dynamically within the personality, this is not a simple model. Jung's ideas have been made accessible (Myers and Myers 1995) and they have been applied extensively in management education, careers guidance, counselling and personal development. They have not yet been systematically applied to informal/non-formal learning in cultural, heritage or outdoor environments. Much remains to be done. Psychological type theory might explain why performance improves (and greater pleasure or satisfaction felt) on some occasions when compared with apparently similar ones.

When I looked back at the notes made at the time of my landmark visit to Tate Modern, some years later, I was struck by the way I had described the event in the 'voice' characteristic of my type. Reviewing the writing again now, I am aware that, during that afternoon I was spending time in a familiar, preferred way. But I had also done that many times before and felt contentment, relaxation and general enjoyment. Yet, it had not precipitated any significant change in either my behaviour or my thinking about looking at art objects in galleries. Those occasions were pleasant sociable afternoons. This one went well beyond that.

What seems to have been different is that it also posed a greater degree of challenge which became sharply focused on a particular Matisse painting. My attention was concentrated by the right question, about the right object, put in the right way, by the right person. I stretched myself, taking a risk in answering it. I realized at that moment that I wanted to be the kind of person who could look at complex pictures and make meaning for myself. Although this came as a bit of a shock, I was used to similar, defining realizations occurring in the middle of activity. Such moments may be thought of as 'epiphanies'. People who share my psychological preferences tend to want to experience the world in order to understand it, so we are more likely to experience insight in *action* rather than when engaged in *reflection*. I had momentarily grasped how it might feel to be able to relate to art objects in this way. I realized for the first time that people like me could do it. I also knew that if I wanted to get that tiny thrill again I had to adapt my behaviour and reconsider some of the views I had tacitly held about the way people learn to look at art.

Transformative learning theory has been extensively refined and critiqued since 1978 when Mezirow published a study of women returners to community college in the United States (Mezirow 1978, cited by Mezirow and Associates 2000). While that focus seems very different, I think the approach it generated makes a contribution to the process of appreciating what happened to me. Mezirow was interested in learning which could overcome tendencies towards conservative thinking in adulthood. We tend to expect that youth is a time of rapid change (physical, cognitive, emotional and social) the pace of such change generally slows down in maturity. Mezirow presents transformative learning as subjecting habitual ways of thinking to critical re-examination, in order to see if these ways of thinking remain fit for purpose. He characterizes learning as having the potential to emancipate adults from restricted, prejudiced or otherwise inadequate assumptions. Such transformations tend to occur when learners are faced by 'disorienting dilemmas' and have an opportunity to develop new perspectives in dialogue with their peers.

When presented with the challenge (to say what the painting was about) I was confronted by my own disorienting dilemma. I could avoid the challenge by not making a serious attempt at interpretation or I could give it my best shot and run the risk of looking stupid. *The Moroccans* is a powerful and richly complex image. Had I visited the exhibition alone, I might have been overwhelmed by it or ignored it altogether. Claire, in posing this question about that painting, was crucial to the transformative power of the event. In other words, not just the object itself, or the question, but also the person influenced my response. At that moment, my amiable companion was transformed into a trusted teacher. I believed she had selected a challenge for which I was ready, so I went for it. In making my choice I relied upon my preferred cognitive function (intuition) in the extraverted attitude, resolved a dilemma and took the first step towards belonging to a new social network. The precise formula for this mix was specific to me and to that moment. A spark had been struck. I was for a while dependent for the vitality of my learning, like a new-born, on Claire's ongoing investment of time and expertise. Experienced teachers may recognize what has been called the 'teachable moment'. It cannot be forced but it can be either squandered or cherished. Communication channels are open and the learner is ready to respond. The nurturing of such moments so they can grow is vital. Anyone who does it occupies, even temporarily, the role of teacher. You may be able to recall being such a midwife at the birth of a new interest or understanding in learners. Many teachers identify such times as the moments when they recognized a talent for teaching. They may continue to motivate teachers, in any context, in the practice of their craft.

Lave and Wenger (1991) published some influential ideas about socio-cultural influences on adult learning in informal/non-formal environments. Five ethnographic studies of varied forms of 'apprenticeship' provided the research material which prompted their thoughts about adults learning with and from each other. They go beyond theorists who describe the social situation as having an influence on individual cognition (like Vygotsky) when they say that:

> Learning viewed as situated activity has as its central defining characteristic a process that we call *legitimate peripheral participation*. By this we mean to draw attention to the point that learners inevitably participate in communities of practitioners and that the mastery of knowledge and skill requires newcomers to move towards full participation in the socio-cultural practices of a community.
>
> (Lave and Wenger 1991: 29)

Participants learning together are not just individuals who happen to share the same space because it is cheaper or more convenient to do it like that (unless the crudest form of 'crop spraying' is the dominant pedagogy). Knowledge is processed and refined in company with other members of your community. What counts as worthwhile are not just the particular insights or assumptions an individual may come to hold. It is through discourse that learning is shared and meaning is made while membership of a particular community is consolidated.

You may be thinking that this makes sense when training for a career but what has it got to do with learning informally for example, with art objects? As well as being challenged to use my cognitive functions to describe what I thought *The Moroccans* might be about, I was aware that Claire was inviting me to become 'one of us'. In other words, I knew that my companion's identity as an art historian was an important aspect of her sense of self. By posing that question, she was inviting me to take a step towards being a peripheral member of the community of practice within which she has high status. There were many ways this had been gradually developing as we had got to know each other, but that was the moment when I could take a step over the threshold. That is partly why it felt so risky yet so exciting. The dilemma she posed by asking me to tell her what I could see (at this point I did not know the title of the picture) was not just about making sense of paint on canvas, it was also asking if I was ready to identify myself with people like her. If I wanted to do this (which I became aware I did) was I up to the task?

My journal records that a few days later the exhibition was the subject of a television documentary. I did not normally watch art programmes on television but I was curious to see what they did with the show I had just seen. In the middle of this programme the presenter discussed the Matisse picture which had been my challenge. He observed that some contemporary critics agree with the interpretation I had suggested, rather than the traditional scholarship with which Claire was familiar. The surge of pleasure was immense. I had met the first challenge. I had begun to function within a new set of socio-cultural practices as what Lave and Wenger (1991) describe as a 'legitimate peripheral participant'. So I started to look for more such opportunities. I also wondered whether my experience was unusual or common.

A growing interest in looking at art objects sparked my curiosity about gallery visitors in general. It seems that a kind of chemistry between objects and the viewers can sustain attention while perception is organized and decisions made. This sustained concentration upon something when no external pressure requires you to do it, interested me. I wanted to learn more about how it might work. As I did so, I came across work within the arena of museum studies. Not surprisingly, at least some of those professionals who work in museums and galleries are interested in the behaviour and motivation of their visitors.

So, my journey had gone from curiosity about an unusual event in my leisure time to a professional interest in the motivation of visitors to art galleries. I am theorizing in the company of those who practise as non-formal teachers in galleries and museums and other all-age learning environments to try to uncover the conditions which will enable visitors to become learners. We want to understand much more about the interventions which can be made by teachers through face-to-face contact, the design and distribution of materials (hard copy and electronic) and the design and construction of the exhibition or event itself. To do this we need to know the objects of the learning, and the technologies whose potential can be harnessed more effectively. At heart I think teachers are also interested in the learners themselves. I have been focusing upon the way individual difference in cognitive functioning combines with the external factors to ignite in a flame of pleasure. Finally, I can turn attention on to this 'flame'. Perhaps, whereas many people have experienced formal education as pain (or hard labour to avoid the pain they know awaits the less diligent) learning informally or within non-formal environments may be motivated and sustained by pleasure. Let us look at this next.

The relationship between pleasure and learning has gained more general attention as interest in informal/non-formal learning has grown and technology has been harnessed to sustain a huge industry based on the use of C&IT for playing games. A state of heightened awareness, concentration combined with relaxation and pleasure has been described as 'flow' (Csikszentmihalyi 1990). Csikszentmihalyi and Hermanson (1999) propose a link between the importance of a positive state of mind for learning and the characteristics of the 'flow state'. Chess players, rock climbers, dancers, painters, musicians and basketball players were among the subjects for the original research into the motivation which keeps participants involved in demanding activities for which there may be no external reward. When the participants in such diverse activities were asked to describe their personal experience the accounts were strikingly similar. Clear goals linked with the subject's perception of their own capacity to meet the challenge of such goals are essential contributors to the achievement of the feeling of flow. They say of flow experiences that:

> they tend to occur when the opportunities for action in a situation are in balance with the person's abilities . . . If challenges are greater than skills, anxiety results; if skills are greater than challenges, the result is boredom . . . As skills increase, the

challenge of the activity must also increase to continue the state
of flow. The skills involved are those perceived by the individual, however and not necessarily the actual ones . . . Even if
one is involved in an activity that typically induces flow, flow
cannot be attained if one is worried about performance or if
other negative states prevail . . . When goals are clear, feedback
unambiguous, challenges and skills well matched, then all of
one's mind and body becomes completely involved in the
activity. Attention is focused and concentration is so intense
that there is nothing left over to think anything irrelevant or
to worry about problems. In the flow state a person is unaware
of fatigue and the passing of time; hours pass by in what seems
like minutes. This depth of involvement is enjoyable and
intrinsically rewarding

> (Csikszentmihalyi and Hermanson 1999: 150–1)

When I read Csikszentmihalyi's description of flow, I recognized immediately that it was similar to the way I felt at Tate Modern on that May
afternoon. I also realized that it was a familiar experience. Previously,
I had expected to get it, for example when sailing a dinghy, dancing or
scuba diving. I had never before felt that way, when looking at pictures
or undertaking essentially cognitive tasks. I thought that only physically
demanding activities enabled me to feel like that. It was good to discover that the experience had already been quite extensively researched
and described as flow. The research indicates (and my experience con-
curs) that it is the subtle and unstable relationship between challenge
and capacity which triggers flow. The activity which will induce flow
can vary hugely (the mix of active and reflective elements may vary considerably) though there may be an indication that some people (possibly those who share certain psychological preferences) are more likely
to experience it than others.

The aesthetic experience, defined as 'an intense involvement of
attention in response to a visual stimulus for no other reason than to
sustain the interaction' (Csikszentmihalyi and Robinson 1990: 178) can
be compared to a climber's experience on a rockface in this respect. 'Flow'
can occur for climbers with any degree of expertise but it will be triggered by different combinations of elements. If the pitch is too severe
the climber will be anxious (possibly resulting in the avoidance of any
such jeopardy again), if it is too easy, the experience of boredom may
lead to disengagement. If the match is good, then climbers may feel challenged, absorbed, in harmony with themselves, their environment and
their companions. They are deeply fulfilled and will want to repeat the
experience. This description precisely matched the way I felt when

deeply absorbed in trying to interpret the complexity and subtlety of *The Moroccans*. The desire to repeat the experience ensured that I was motivated to see more. I had to know if I could rise to the challenge again and if I did, would I feel the charge of excitement which was so wonderfully enjoyable?

Research into learning styles and pedagogy (Coffield et al. 2004) indicated that learning is most strongly linked to the time spent engaged in it (time on task) and the provision of effective feedback. Informal learning has no certainty of externally provided feedback through rewards or punishments. So we might infer that the contexts which will have the richest potential for informal learning are those with 'autotelic' properties built into them. In other words they are self-rewarding. In order to get reward (often in terms of a sense of pleasure) over a period of time (the individual disconnected moments are known as 'micro flow'), learners must be developing their expertise and the activity must have the potential to become more challenging. Such competence may be in terms of knowledge and cognition, physical skills or all of them.

The designers of computer games exploit many of the aspects of flow in the attributes of their products. Individuals find that, when playing computer games, the feedback on performance is often unequivocal; the level of difficulty can be selected or rises automatically as performance improves, rewards are immediate (e.g. by sounds, extra 'lives', various forms of tradable currency or length of time the player may continue in the game) and satisfaction is felt as performance improves. In this context flow seems to be available on demand. Players have their satisfaction guaranteed. I am not saying it is necessarily a 'soft' option when compared with the other kinds of activities known to induce flow. I do wonder, however, if it can be more isolating and less likely to prove to be in any enduring sense meaningful. Such questions can deteriorate into issues of taste (rather like the sterile 1960s debate about the relative merits of Beethoven and the Beatles). Perhaps there is a way forward when we look again at Pointon's comments upon pleasure and knowledge when looking at art. She says:

> Acknowledging the importance of enjoying something does not, of course, preclude a historical analysis of the object that is arousing pleasure. It might in fact be more pleasurable if we know more about the object we are viewing. Moreover, pleasure is not a simple matter. The arousal of our senses – and how we recognize and register it – is itself open to interrogation. It is also historically located. Why we like particular characteristics of certain sorts of objects at any one time is not simply the result of our genes or our own particular personalities but is determined

by values promoted within the society of which we are a part. So, while no one seeks to underestimate the importance of sensuous and instinctual responses to art objects, the notion that the sensuous is undermined by the intellectual is a legacy from a period in the past which promoted art as an alternative to thought.

(Pointon 1997: 6)

When visiting a gallery alone (or selecting a computer game to play) that which is familiar may be very attractive. I should not have recognized for myself that I would gain so much from seeing the Matisse Picasso exhibition. Nor would I have asked myself the question about *The Moroccans* which was the start of a newly intense enjoyment found in looking at art; and beginning to understand something of the history and cultural significance of its display in galleries, churches, domestic and public spaces. Even now, while often gaining something from an aesthetic encounter, I am aware that flow eludes me much of the time. It is most likely to occur when I visit a gallery with Claire, my companion on that transformative occasion. Questioning her significance in the event led me to investigate the complex relationship between teacher and learner outside the classroom. This includes both informal learning (where the teaching is largely serendipitous if available at all) and non-formal contexts. Having spent some time considering the informal learning which took place during a social visit to a gallery, I want to look at an example from the non-formal context. A church choir provides an all-age environment which comes together to produce music for weekly worship but is also a rich source of non-formal learning for all its participants.

Teaching outside the classroom

By teaching 'outside the classroom' I mean not only beyond dedicated physical spaces which house learners while they receive formal instruction but also outside the social conventions, sanctions and inducements which operate within formal learning. Can the potential of non-formal and informal learning to contribute substantially to a lifelong learning agenda be realized without replicating the restrictive conditions which can characterize formal learning? These conditions may resonate with negative experiences of learning earlier in life and so inhibit the potential for flow. In other words, is it possible to retain the creativity and distinctiveness of learning outside classrooms while making it more accessible, powerful and recognizable? Meeting such a challenge requires well-informed action at the macro/policy, meso/professional and micro/individual levels. Getting it wrong will squander a significant resource. How should teachers set about the task?

Teaching in this context takes many forms but many of them may be understood through the metaphor of the teacher as guide and fellow traveller. Parts of the journey will be undertaken by learners on their own (and it is an attribute of mature learners that they can do so without faltering) but learning is rarely undertaken entirely alone. It can be optimized by companionship. Another person helps us to tune in to the pleasure which the situation can provide and recognize what it will take to sustain and increase such pleasure. They may significantly enhance the sense of achievement or be able to encourage us to persist when times are hard. Sometimes they contribute what could be described as disciplinary expertise (the choir's conductor, the canoeist willing to immerse herself in cold water to pull me up at the right moment and Claire, my companion for the gallery visits) but if they have such expertise it is communicated differently outside the formal context. Their expertise becomes a resource at the disposal of the learners not an excuse for the exercise of personal power.

Although Csikszentmihalyi and Robinson (1990) had interviewed experts when discovering the characteristics of the aesthetic experience, the description resonated strikingly with my experience of being a novice in the safe and stimulating company of an off-duty expert or teacher. Novices often need assistance if they are to locate themselves within the illusive flow zone. Alone in a rich environment the very abundance of potential learning opportunities may be bewildering or even intimidating. We can feel that everyone else knows more than we do; that this place is 'not for the likes of us'. The fear of embarrassment through exposure of our ignorance is very real. Unless an atmosphere of emotional safety exists, adults rarely risk showing themselves up. Such anxiety can prompt learners to flee from the very place where they need to be. In non-formal learning responsibility for the creation of the safe, supportive environment may be shared, expertise located in many of the learners as well as in a leader. The church choir I mentioned earlier is such a place for its members. Years of regular observation provide the basis for this brief account of the way it works.

There has been a choir at the church in the village for as long as anyone can remember. One or two of its current members sang in it man and boy, sustaining their involvement for more then 40 years. Girls and women were permitted to join the singers on equal terms as recently as 1999, when the practice of relying on boy trebles was discontinued. Boys are still welcome but the mainstay of the top line is now women's voices. The age range is currently 15 to 70+ years of age. It is perhaps this mixture of ages which makes it an interesting case study. Contemporary English society provides relatively few learning opportunities for women, men and children to work and learn together. Within the choir's membership there are also various family groups; currently these include husband + wife, wife + husband + son; father + sons + sister + mother-in-law. Similar combinations in the past mean that grown-up children contribute to an outer circle of adults who sing when they are visiting the family home. Including the regular singers and the occasional contributors the choir consists of around 35 members. Most weeks there will be between 20 and 25 singers who rehearse and/or sing during the Sunday worship.

The choir's primary function is to enhance worship by leading congregational singing and singing anthems and more musically demanding settings of liturgy for the congregation to listen to. This distinguishes it from those choirs which exist primarily for the musical education of their members or to perform concerts for audiences of music lovers. The choir could not succeed if its members stopped learning but such learning fulfils an auxiliary function. This choir is a good example of an all-age non-formal learning environment.

Learning within this context means something slightly different to each person. The theoretical perspectives which emerged from my enquiry into my own informal learning in an art gallery also apply to this example of non-formal learning by a group. I will discuss each one briefly, taking them in the same order as they are discussed above. Individual differences in cognitive preference are observable within this group learning together. When structuring the rehearsal session, which generally lasts about 75 minutes, the conductor includes activities which recognize the energy flow differences for introverts and extraverts. For example when learning a new piece extraverts will tend to be ready to try singing it straight away and learn it by engagement through frequent repetition and discussion of what is going well and what is not yet correct. Introverts by contrast may well prefer to listen as it is performed and if they read music, they will be likely to want to have the score in advance so that they can prepare alone before being asked to do anything. Extraverts may enjoy working on a range of contrasting pieces in each rehearsal while introverts might like it better when they can concentrate on one or two pieces in some depth.

Sensing types will tend to learn most effectively by the process that musicians sometimes call 'note-bashing'. In other words, they enjoy working systematically, mastering detail in order to facilitate incremental progression. Those who enjoy an intuitive preference will generally want to acquire an overall impression of the whole piece before doing any detailed work on any of the parts. They are very comfortable when the conductor decides to begin work with the end or middle sections of the piece to be sung, while this can seem disorienting for the sensers, unless they are given good reasons for the logic of the choice. Thinking and feeling judgements may not directly impact on the technical aspects of the rehearsal but they are very important differences in the ways the singers approach the general management of the choir and the way decisions are made about how it fulfils its function. Thinking types may for example express frustration if they think some choir members are not showing sufficient commitment to rehearse and sing in regular services. Their feeling-type colleagues may seem more willing to accept that all individuals are doing the best they can with the different circumstances of their lives. They may occasionally seem surprisingly harsh however if let down unexpectedly or should they ever feel that their own contribution is taken for granted or in some other sense that their goodwill has been abused. In non-formal learning environments these differences (among others which we might also discuss if space permitted) can have an important impact on the success of the whole endeavour.

If the conductor has his own particular set of psychological preferences and always structures the learning in ways which suit himself, at least some members of the choir are likely to find themselves always working in ways which do not feel comfortable. At best they will be tired and not enjoy the experience. At worst they will give up. An obvious musical analogy would be if the conductor or teacher in the group was himself a tenor and always spent more time ensuring the tenors were happy and ignored the needs and interests of all the alto singers. By contrast with such a negative example, when the rehearsal has been structured to include opportunities for the different preferences to be accessed by the learners, many of them comment that despite working hard they feel positively energized. Singing is an activity which increases oxygen uptake and can release the hormones which prompt feelings of wellbeing, but this physiological explanation does not seem to tell the whole story. Working within our psychological preferences tends to boost confidence and enhance performance. This confidence also improves performance in the singing and triggers a virtuous circle of pleasure, success and increased work-rate. We shall return to pleasure in a few minutes.

Moving on to consider the relevance of an appreciation of transformative learning in this context takes us away from the technicalities of the way rehearsals are structured to acquire musical expertise in the singing of particular pieces and recognizes two things. First, that participation in this kind of group has the capacity to change or reinforce the way its members think about themselves and those around them. Transformative learning tends to concentrate on changes to long-held ways of thinking, so that they are replaced by new perspectives which are in a sense more adult and fully formed. Participation in the choir means more than just singing different items. It involves occupying a new place in the life of the community whose purposes it serves. The Church of England has many traditions which make such transformations visible and tangible. This is a robed choir. All members wear black cassock and white surplice when they are taking part in worship and sit in a different part of the building. These changes in dress, behaviour and position represent the choir's commitment to its overall purpose. This is universally valued more highly than the normal desire of musicians to be valued as individual performers who are admired for their personal talent or expertise. Membership of this particular choir (and many others like it who operate within a similar tradition) requires singers to learn to think differently about what they do week by week. Most of them find it immensely satisfying and liberating as they do so.

The transformative potential of the choir's learning is deeply related to the social participation in its shared responsibility. New members are inducted through a recognizable process of legitimate peripheral participation into the 'community of practice'. In Chapter 4 I described how a novice singer was surrounded by old-timers and gradually learned not only how to sing the notes but also how to 'become a bass'. The small group of singers, whose voices fit each one of the four parts which make up an equal voice choir in western choral music, share a common identity as a subset of the whole choir. People belong to a part as well as to the choir as a whole. Much of the humour which makes rehearsals enjoyable as well as productive arises from inter-part rivalry. Always good natured (in this particular choir but not in all cases) it is easily recognizable as an essential element in the motivational mix. Transitions between parts may be a sign of maturation. Because boys' voices break as they mature into men, the transition from treble to one of the lower parts is an overt one. The boys move physically from sitting with the women sopranos to join one of the other three parts which include adult men. Girls may move from soprano to alto, but the transition is not inevitable nor is it imbued with a similar cultural significance.

Finally, does singing induce flow? Csikszentmihalyi (1990) is clear that it has the potential to do so. Members of the choir who are not familiar with the concept of flow describe occasions when they have experienced the characteristic feelings. They often say (during rehearsals, so the learning experience can itself be the source of flow) that they lost track of the time, felt completely caught up in the activity, felt at one with themselves and each other, completely forgot other issues which had been worrying them and wanted the sensation to go on for ever. It is, however, worth noticing that singing can also be the source of extreme anxiety, discomfort, embarrassment and social isolation. In other words it is important to remember that no activity guarantees the flow state. The dynamic relationship between the challenge presented and the participant's perception of her/his ability to rise to that challenge is fundamental. To get the most from a situation, learners must feel they are in control themselves and/or working with others who they trust to set an appropriate challenge. Passivity and/or fear make flow unlikely to occur.

In this non-formal learning environment the members of the choir rely upon each other to ensure that they can meet challenges which many of them recognize might be beyond them in other circumstances. It is not simply that they have varieties of musical competence distributed among the singers but also that they share the common status as equal contributors to this work of service to their community. Older and younger singers are liberated from the contemporary, market-driven motivation to segmentation, competition and isolation. Here, age, taste in clothes or politics or anything else which divides members of society becomes more or less irrelevant. Sustaining your vocal part is what counts and you stand or fall together. There is no 'exotelic' reward or threat to your performance in this environment. This is genuinely 'autotelic' (self-rewarding). Effective teaching here requires that the contributions of all are recognized for the good of all. Power is never exercised with a heavy hand. Learning and teaching exist in harmony without anyone or anything else checking-up to see it happens. For learners of all ages this is both truly grown-up and child-like in its approach to the task.

Conclusion

Early in this chapter I proposed that 'the work of teachers in these [informal/non-formal] contexts has received less critical attention and practical exposition within the literature than that of their colleagues in formal educational contexts . . . This work deserves consideration for five reasons'. In concluding let us check those reasons again. They are:

- Growing significance in social policy
- Demand for recognition of life experience in formal study
- The benefit of shared good practice
- Opportunities for innovation and expertise transfer
- Conceptual problems and ambiguities require solving.

To put it another way, if the best use is to be made of all opportunity for adult learning, then teaching needs to be understood more broadly. This chapter has started the process of thinking about the ways teachers intervene to support learning events, activities and experiences to assist the learner to exploit the potential of the situation more fully. Effective teachers adapt theory and practice to work in formal, non-formal and informal contexts for the benefit of their learners and themselves.

The potential of a place, situation, encounter or experience is catalysed when a teacher's vision, technical expertise and values interact with an active or latent expectation of learning. The teacher working without educational institutions is liberated from many of the constraints which occupy much of the energy of those exercising their talents within organizations dedicated to learning. The capacity released is available for creative, multidimensional (and sometimes plain wacky) approaches to enabling and sustaining learning. It may be that under such circumstances the 'flow' state is most likely to occur for teachers and learners. Society has an opportunity to harvest such bounty if it can do so without exhausting the supply or contaminating the source. Perhaps (as anthropologists are currently concerned to learn from remote communities without jeopardizing them, as once they might have done) mainstream practitioners can explore the teaching and learning which takes place in the unorthodox corners of the educational world without colonizing it. The future of educational development depends upon those inspiring teachers who find a space to engage with learners in exciting ways, with strange material; doing new things and thinking new thoughts. Much of this takes place outdoors, in museums, galleries, libraries and archives, hospitals, studios, theatres, workplaces, families, leisure and fitness clubs, faith communities, village halls, self-help groups like the National Childbirth Trust and all manner of other locations. Teachers in formal environments can be encouraged, stimulated and challenged by those operating outside the boundary. However, people working outside the formal context may have a partial or unformed sense of their own professional expertise responsibilities, ethics and opportunities. Genuine exchange of understanding through shared practice is likely to enable learners to transfer their knowledge more readily from one context to another and help teachers to practise more innovatively.

Look around and you will find people seeking out the joy of being taught and recognizing for themselves those who are called to teach. Everyone will benefit if we can sustain this pleasure and harness its energy.

Recognizing 'flow' as 'the state in which people are so involved in an activity that nothing else seems to matter' (Csikszentmihalyi 1990: 4) is useful when we think about the potential for enhancing learning in any context. Effective teaching, whoever is providing it, will focus attention on the significant elements of the situation. It will help learners to eliminate background 'noise' which distracts and disrupts the ability of each individual to control what happens in the consciousness moment by moment. Teachers operate at this micro-level but they are also concerned to create environments, manage systems and enable learners to reflect critically upon performance in one situation so that they may take responsibility for themselves in applying their success as learners in a new context. If the potential for learning in informal or non-formal environments is to be actualized, teachers need to be active across sectors, contexts and environments. Teaching has never been a more important or pleasurable work.

7 Conclusion
The professional character
of the teacher

At first glance, the chapters of this book are largely devoted to an exploration of aspects of the practice of *teaching* adult learners; yet in so doing, they are frequently threaded with references to the character of the *teacher*. Bearing in mind the huge range of activities entailed in the practice of teaching and the myriad contexts in which it may take place, it should become clear that a truly comprehensive analysis of teaching method is impossible in these short pages. However, in selecting key practical issues for discussion and endeavouring to illustrate relevant points of interest, both conceptual and applied, I have tried to convey the essence of the way a professional teacher might think. In other words, rather than seeking to give a 'how to' manual of teaching practice, I have sought to give a flavour of the concerns and values which define a teacher's professionalism. In this conclusion, therefore, it seems appropriate to draw these thoughts together more explicitly, and sketch the key outlines of the teacher's professional character.

The idea of 'professional character'

The notion of 'character' is a helpful one. The *Oxford English Dictionary* definition makes clear that the word refers not only to the 'essential peculiarity' or sum of the qualities which distinguish a thing, but also the 'personality or "part" assumed by an actor on the stage'. In exploring the idea of the teacher's professional character, therefore, we are not seeking to define what a teacher 'must' be, but rather to describe the qualities which enable us to recognize when an individual is playing a teacher's role. A professional 'character' is thus not strictly the same as an 'identity'. In the theatre, for example, the actor's personal appearance, attributes and experience largely define and shape the character they portray; there is no 'right' way to play a particular character; each actor offers their own interpretation. In the same way, in offering a sketch of the teacher's professional character, I do not seek to prescribe a particular form of teaching. A character is a framework of values and goals set in a specific context. The individual is left to bring the character alive.

Assuming the professional character of the teacher means assuming a specific set of obligations and standards, but one within which an individual's unique background, expertise and creativity are free to flourish.

This approach is particularly apposite in the context of adult learning. As we have already noted, in addition to those who have made conscious choices to follow teaching careers, many mid-career professionals who never foresaw that teaching would form a part of their daily practice are also required to take responsibility for the learning of others as a secondary aspect of their main field of interest. Reference to the notion of the professional character of the teacher, which is put on or taken off when a person steps on or off the teacher's 'stage', is a helpful way of envisaging the combination of professional obligations which a person must manage.

The notion of 'character' also has value in emphasizing the holistic nature of the development required to become a professional teacher. Although, as teachers, we can – and do – all benefit from periodically learning a new 'trick' or two throughout our careers, the fundamental development of our professional practice is not done piecemeal. Becoming a professional teacher requires more than the mechanistic accumulation of new techniques: it is about the consistent application of a set of core values.

An ability to conceptualize the professional character of the teacher is thus of value in translating the themes of this book into daily practice. As we saw in Chapter 3, general recognition of the professional character of the teacher plays an important part in motivating people to meet the various challenges that the practice of teaching poses. Moreover, I am certain that readers will be – and probably already have been – faced by challenges unique to their circumstances, not falling clearly within the examples or contexts I have expressly explored. Analysing these challenges within the framework of the following portrait should, however, provide some inspiration as to the way to proceed.

Defining the professional character of the teacher

The essence of the teacher's professional character can be defined very succinctly. Professional teachers seek to communicate their field of knowledge to the learner with fidelity and accuracy, within the context of their professional ethics, and in such a way that the learner is nurtured, supported and able to develop. In the light of the themes explored earlier in this book, we can illustrate this definition by reference to three principal characteristics.

A teacher acts with professional agency

It is a commonplace that teachers are something more than a mere resource to be accessed by learners. They make a central contribution to the effectiveness of learning in all contexts, and must be actively engaged in all aspects of the learning process. Not just a matter of time spent 'covering the content', we have seen that this includes a practical concern for the learners which extends before and after their arrival in the classroom. Time in the classroom should be 'eventful', with a structured use of relevant activities to break the ice, support and sustain core learning, and to consolidate the work which has taken place.

Teachers should be active managers of the learning environment, optimizing it for the needs of their learners where possible and overcoming environmental disadvantages where necessary. In certain circumstances, where their professional judgement indicates that thrifty subsistence has slipped into poverty, they must have the courage to address environmental deficiencies with their parent institution in a respectful but resolute manner. Teachers should make use of appropriate technology and resources, on their own behalf or collaboratively as necessary, even developing or adapting them where it may further the learning process.

Teachers should also play a role in managing learner expectations, especially when teaching adults. Their duty of care for *all* the learners in their charge, their ethical obligation of fidelity to the subject matter, and the necessary demands of practicality mean that their professional assessment of appropriate practice can sometimes depart from individual expectations. Learners sometimes require thoughtful assistance in appreciating the reasonable bounds of a teacher's efforts. This process is also partly a matter of enlightened self-interest: a teacher's assistance in developing the learners' ability to recognize positive teaching experiences may reflect well upon them in turn.

A teacher acts ethically

This aspect of the teacher's character poses the question of the extent of their ethical obligations. Obviously, individual teachers may bring individual ethical perspectives to their work. However, professional teaching entails commitment to certain core values, which contribute significantly to the definition of the teacher's character. The ethical basis of the teacher's profession is essential: teaching and learning cannot flourish in a climate of suspicion; mutual trust and respect are essential to a learning relationship. Indeed, teaching and learning become more challenging as greater diversity means that there may be less common understanding and shared experience upon which to build. Stressing the

ethical basis of the teacher's professional character is an important measure to counteract this trend.

Teachers maintain a sustained interest in their own practice, as a basis
for an active commitment to professional development. This may take
many forms, but should include the assumption of responsibility for personal updating, evaluation of performance, and reasonable adjustment
to systemic change in working conditions. Teachers may choose to find
a suitable method of evidencing their own competent practice, in the
light of the interests of their employer, their profession and society.

Teachers are obliged to act with fidelity to their subject matter and
the interests of their learners. In this context, teachers have a responsibility for the care and wellbeing of the learners, but moderated by
the detachment warranted by the professional relationship that exists
between them. Teachers must act with respect for the knowledge,
beliefs and experience of the learners. This may sometimes require a sens-
itive approach to teaching which takes into account the individuality
of the learner, as well as the dynamic of the group as a whole.

A teacher exercises professional judgement

To a great extent, the key resource which the teacher has to 'trade' with
their learners is their depth of knowledge and experience, which is mani-
fested through the exercise of professional judgement. The most obvious example of this characteristic is the teacher's thoughtful approach
to the use of assessment and feedback, broadly conceived to include
the exercise of professional judgement for the purposes of motivating
learners, supporting them in their progress, recording their achievement,
and certifying their membership of restricted communities.

The ability to exercise professional judgement is also a corollary of the
teacher's practice as an active agent in the learning process, a characteristic we have already identified. Often informed by an understanding
of the pedagogic or disciplinary issues, teachers recognize and form
opinions about the needs of learners, and act accordingly.

Conclusion

The portrait above does not necessarily mean that teachers will be
aware of fulfilling any or all of these functions. For example, we have
noted that in certain non-formal and informal contexts, people may not
even be aware that they have stepped into the role of 'the teacher' at
all. Similarly, they may not remain in the role consistently, or on a
regular basis. Although such uncertainty or such a variation is deeply

troubling in a formal learning context, it may be a necessary consequence of the negotiated nature of other forms of learning. I hope that the flexible 'character'-driven approach to teaching offered here should illustrate that there are rather more teachers about than we might think.

Similarly, the portrait that I have presented demonstrates that teachers are *engaged* with the world – and that our instinct, as teachers, is to reflect upon and modify (where appropriate) our practice in the light of our experience. Accordingly, teachers are themselves transformed through the process of teaching. To be a teacher really means to be a learner. And in a time when education for all ages is said to have come of age, there has never been a better time to learn – and to teach.

References

Anderson, D. (1999) *A Commonwealth: Museums in the Learning Age – A Report to the Department of Culture, Media and Sport*. London: The Stationery Office.

Barker, E., Webb, N. and Woods, K. (1999) *The Changing Status of the Artist*. New Haven, CT: Yale University Press in association with the Open University.

Belenky, M.F., Clinchy, B.M., Goldberger, N.R. and Tarule, J.M. (1986) *Women's Ways of Knowing*. New York: Basic Books.

Biggs, J. and Tang, C. (2007) *Teaching for Quality Learning at University*, 3rd edn. Buckingham: SRHE and Open University Press.

Brookfield, S. (1986) *Understanding and Facilitating Adult Learning*. San Francisco, CA: Jossey-Bass.

Brookfield, S. (2005) *The Power of Critical Theory for Adult Learning and Teaching*. Maidenhead: Open University Press.

Cathcart, T. and Klein, D. (2007) *Plato and a Platypus Walk into a Bar . . . : Understanding Philosophy through Jokes*. New York: Abrams.

Chatterjee, H.J. (ed.) (2008) *Touch in Museums: Policy and Practice in Object Handling*. Oxford: Berg.

Coffield, F., Moseley, D., Hall, E. and Ecclestone, K. (2004) *Learning Styles and Pedagogy in Post-16 Learning: A Systematic and Critical Review*. London: Learning and Skills Research Centre.

Cowling, E. (2002) *Interpreting Matisse Picasso*. London: Tate Publishing.

Cranton, P. (1989) *Planning Instruction for Adult Learners*. Toronto: Wall & Thompson.

Csikszentmihalyi, M. (1990) *Flow*. New York: Harper & Row.

Csikszentmihalyi, M. and Hermanson, K. (1999) Intrinsic motivation in museums. Why does one want to learn? In E. Hooper-Greenhill (ed.), *The Educational Role of the Museum*, 2nd edn. London: Routledge.

Csikszentmihalyi, M. and Robinson, R.E. (1990) *The Art of Seeing: An Interpretation of the Aesthetic Encounter*. Malibu, CA: J.P. Getty Museum.

Cullen, J., Hadjivassilion, K., Hamilton, E., et al. (2002) *Review of Current Pedagogic Research and Practice in the Fields of Post-compulsory Education and Lifelong Learning*. London: Tavistock Institute.

Fox, D. (1983) Personal theories of teaching and learning. *Studies in Higher Education*, 8(2): 151–63.

Freire, P. (1996) *Pedagogy of the Oppressed*, 2nd edn. London: Penguin.

Gardner, H. (2006) *The Development and Education of the Mind: The Selected Works of Howard Gardner*. London: Routledge.

Gilligan, C. (1982) *In a Different Voice*: *Psychological Theory and Women's Development*. Cambridge, MA: Harvard University Press.

Goleman, D. (1995) *Emotional Intelligence: Why It Can Matter More Than IQ*. London: Bloomsbury.

Gore, J.M. (1993) *The Struggle for Pedagogies: Critical and Feminist Discourses as Regimes of Truth*. London: Routledge.

Jung, C.G. (1971) *Psychological Types*, translated by H.G. Baynes, revised by R.F.C. Hull. London: Routledge & Kegan Paul.

Knowles, M. (1980) *The Modern Practice of Adult Education: From Pedagogy to Andragogy*, 2nd edn. Englewood Cliffs, NJ: Prentice Hall.

Knowles, M. (ed.) (1984) *Andragogy in Action: Applying Modern Principles of Adult Education*. San Francisco, CA: Jossey-Bass.

Knowles, M. (1990) *The Adult Learner: A Neglected Species*, 4th edn. Houston, TX: Gulf.

Knowles, M. (1996) Andragogy: An emerging technology for adult learning. In R. Edwards, A. Hanson and P. Raggatt (eds) *Boundaries of Adult Learning: Adult Learning, Education and Training*. London: Routledge.

Kolb, D.A. (1984) *Experiential Learning: Experience as the Source of Learning and Development*. Englewood Cliffs, NJ: Prentice Hall.

Lave, J. and Wenger, E. (1991) *Situated Learning, Legitimate Peripheral Participation*. Cambridge: Cambridge University Press.

Maslow, A. (1968) *Toward a Psychology of Being*. New York: Van Nostran Rheinold.

Maslow, A. (1970) *Motivation and Personality*, 2nd edn. New York: Harper & Row.

Mezirow, J. (1978) *Education for Perspective Transformation: Women Re-entry Programmes in Community College*. New York: Teachers College, Columbia University.

Mezirow, J. and Associates (2000) *Learning as Transformation: Critical Perspectives on a Theory in Progress*. San Francisco, CA: Jossey-Bass.

Myers, I.B. and Myers, P.B. (1995) *Gifts Differing: Understanding Personality Type*, 2nd edn. Palo Alto, CA: Davies-Black.

National Committee of Inquiry into Higher Education (1997) *Higher Education in the Learning Society* (Dearing Report). London: HMSO.

Oosthuizen, S. (2002) *Probably the Shortest Introduction to Assessing Adult Students in the World*. Cambridge: Institute of Continuing Education, University of Cambridge.

Phillips, A. (1994) *On Kissing, Tickling and Being Bored: Psychoanalytic Essays on the Unexamined Life*. London: Faber & Faber.

Pointon, M. (1997) *History of Art: A Student's Handbook*, 4th edn. London: Routledge.

Porter, R. (2003) *Flesh in the Age of Reason*. London: Penguin.

Prown, J.D. (1993) The truth of material culture: History or fiction? In S. Lubar and W.D. Kingery (eds), *History from Things: Essays on Material Culture*. Washington, DC: Smithsonian Institution Press.

Pye, E. (ed.) (2007) *The Power of Touch: Handling Objects in Museum and Heritage Contexts*. London: Institute of Archaeology, University College London and Left Coast Press.

Rogers, A. (2007) *Teaching Adults*, 3rd edn. Maidenhead: Open University Press.

Rogers, C. (1969) *Freedom to Learn: A View of What Education Might Become*. Columbus, OH: Merrill.

Rogers, C. and Freiberg, H. (1994) *Freedom to Learn*, 3rd edn. Columbus, OH: Merrill.

Rogers, J. (2001) *Adults Learning*, 4th edn. Maidenhead: Open University Press.

Rust, C., Price, M. and O'Donovan, B. (2003) Improving students' learning by developing their understanding of assessment criteria and processes. *Assessment and Evaluation in Higher Education* 28(2): 147–64.

Salmon, G. (2002) *E-tivities: The Key to Active Online Learning*. London: Routledge.

Salzberger-Wittenberg, I., Williams, G. and Osborne, E. (1999) *The Emotional Experience of Learning and Teaching*. London: Karnac.

Schön, D. (1991) *The Reflective Practitioner*. Aldershot: Ashgate.

Schuller, T., Preston, J., Hammond, C., Brassett-Grundy, A. and Bynner, J. (2004) *The Benefits of Learning: The Impact of Education on Health on Family Life and Social Capital*. London: RoutledgeFalmer.

Skelton, A. (2005) *Understanding Teaching Excellence in Higher Education: Towards a Critical Approach*. Abingdon: Routledge.

Tennant, M. (2006) *Psychology and Adult Learning*, 3rd edn. Abingdon: Routledge.

Tight, M. (2002) *Key Concepts in Adult Education and Training*. London: RoutledgeFalmer.

Tusting, K. and Barton, D. (2006) *Models of Adult Learning: A Literature Review*. Leicester: NIACE.

Unit for the Development of Adult Continuing Education (UDACE) (1989) *Understanding Competence*. Leicester: UDACE.

Walters, J. and Gardner, H. (1986) The crystallizing experience: Discovering an intellectual gift. In R.J. Sternberg and J.E. Davidson (eds) *Conceptions of Giftedness*. New York: Cambridge University Press.

Waxenegger, A. (on behalf of the ADD LIFE Consortium) (ed.) (2008) *The ADD LIFE European Tool Kit for Developing Intergenerational Learning in Higher Education*. Graz, Austria: ADD LIFE Consortium.

Wenger, E. (1998) *Communities of Practice: Learning, Meaning and Identity*. Cambridge: Cambridge University Press.

Winter, R. (1989) Learning from Experience: Principles and Practice in Action-Research. London: Falmer Press.

Working Group on Vocational Qualifications (WGVQ) (1986) *Review of Vocational Qualifications in England and Wales*. London: HMSO.

Youell, B. (2005) Assessment, evaluation and inspection in schools. *Journal of Infant Observation* 8(1): 59-68.

Zukas, M. and Malcolm, J. (2002) Pedagogies for lifelong learning: Building bridges or building walls? In R. Harrison, F. Reeve, A. Hanson and J. Clarke (eds), *Supporting Lifelong Learning: Vol. 1 – Perspectives on Teaching*. London: RoutledgeFalmer and Open University Press.

Index

Abundance model 12–4, 112, 114
Accommodation 31
Action Research 74
Adult Learning
  policy 59, 60
Anderson, D. 134
Andragogy 14, 86, 139
Anxiety 15, 71, 110, 118, 149, 157
Apprenticeship 32
Assessment 24–5, 48, 50
  competence-Based *See 'Competence'*
  formal 22
  group 103–4, 108, 109
  informal 22
  methods of 84, 98
  peer 90
  purposes of 84–93
Assimilation 31
Attendance 92
Autonomy 2, 16, 25, 86

Barker, E., et al 79
Behaviourism 15–6
Belenky, M., et al 117
Benchmark 84, 90
Bias 93, 98, 131
Biggs, J., and Tang, C. 13
Blog 50
Boredom 149–50
Brookfield, S. 3, 83, 84
Bruner, J. 31

Cathcart, T., and Klein, D. 127
Chatterjee, H. 123
Choir 153–7
Closings 25
Coach 58, 115
Coffield, F., et al 21, 151
Cognitivism 15–7

Communication & Information
  Technology 27–30, 47, 49
  return on investment 49
Competence 64, 92, 103–8
Conditioning 16
Connoisseurship 69, 75, 78, 80
Constructive alignment 13
Constructivism 17, 27, 30–3, 40, 42, 53
  Social 32, 108, 139
Cranton, P. 88
Csikszentmihalyi, M. 144, 149, 150, 153, 158
  and Hermanson, K. 144, 149–50
  and Robinson, R. 150, 153
Cullen, J., et al 5, 6, 56
Culture 124–5, 156
Curators 41, 145

Dearing *See 'National Committee of Inquiry into Higher Education'*
Deficit model 12, 24
Design, instructional 34, 88
Development, Continuing
  Professional 3, 58, 73, 76, 78
Developmentalism, cognitive 31
Dewey, J. 94
Dilemmas, disorienting 146–7
Dualisms 7, 8, 12, 15

E-learning 29–30, 33, 45–53
Emotion 41, 55
Empathy 20, 113
Environments
  all-age learning 149, 154, 157, 164
  analysis of 35
  blended 49, 52

learning 28, 33–45, 120, 122, 162
  formal 135, 139, 158
  informal 135–8, 140–2, 145, 152,
    158–9, 163
  non-formal 135–42, 145, 152–5,
    157–9, 163
  material 29, 47
  outdoor 38, 39, 145
  physical requirements 43
  residential 38
  safety-critical 39, 104
  teaching 22, 44, 124
  virtual learning (VLE) 29, 45,
    47–51, 68
Ethics, professional 11, 38, 49–50,
    60–1, 73, 93, 108, 115, 124,
    158, 161–3
Experience, peak 113, 126
Experiential Learning Cycle 25
Expertise, professional 25

Facilitation 114
Fear *See 'Anxiety'*
Feedback 2, 21–2, 24–6, 77–8, 85,
    88–9, 93, 99, 108, 151
Feminism 117
Flow 118, 126, 149–52, 156–8
Fox, D. 13
Freiberg, H. 113
Freire, P. 117
Freud, S. 94, 119
Fun 118, 126, 127, 128

Gallery 40, 138, 145–6, 149, 158
  Tate Modern 36, 143, 146, 150
Game, computer 46, 151–2
Gardner, H. 115–6
Gilligan, C. 21, 117
Goleman, D. 116
Gore, J.M. 117

Higher Education Academy (HEA) 65,
    67, 72
Higher Education Funding Council
    for England (HEFCE) 66
Hospital, University College 36
Humour 127, 156

Ice-breakers 20
Identity 14
  pedagogic 70
  professional 29, 53, 55
Incrementalism 31
Innovation 52, 137
Institute of Learning and Teaching in
    Higher Education 64, 65
Intelligence, emotional *See 'Goleman,
    Daniel'*
Interest, conflicts of 50

Journal, reflective 82, 109
Judgment, professional 30, 122, 163
Jung, C.G. 94–6, 116, 145

Knowledge
  procedural 16
  propositional 16
Knowles, M. 14, 20, 86
Kolb, D.A. 25, 94

Laboratory, language 41
Lave, J., and Wenger, E. 1, 32, 147–8
Learners
  adult 2, 20
  older 44, 59, 134, 135, 136
Learner-centredness 8, 9, 10, 11, 12
Learning
  Accreditation of Prior 136–7
  Autotelic 151, 157
  definition of 139
  Lifelong 60, 134, 152
  Lifewide 60, 134
  self-directed 2, 16, 20, 25, 86
  Situated 32, 42
  Transformative 117, 146, 155
  Virtual 46
  Work-Based 3, 109
Legislation 49
Lewin, K. 94
Library, British 36, 40, 43, 143
Life, Second 46
Lifelong Learning UK 65

Maslow, A. 111–3, 116
Mentor *See 'Coach'*

Mezirow, J. 117, 146
Moderation, online 33, 48
Moroccans, The 147–8, 151–2
Motivation 63
Museum 40–1, 138, 145, 149, 158
Myers, I.B., and Myers, P.B. 96–7, 145
Myers Briggs Type Indicator ® 94–103, 145–6, 154–5

National Committee of Inquiry into Higher Education 64
National Student Survey 66–9, 80
National Vocational Qualifications (NVQs) 105–6
Needs, hierarchy of 112

Objects
  Material 33, 146
  Virtual 33
Oosthuizen, S. 82

Participants
  'conscripted' 20–1
  Volunteer 20
Participation 33
  legitimate peripheral 1, 147–8, 156
Pavlov, I.P. 15
Pedagogy 36, 37, 41, 50, 53, 111
Personality, theories of 81, 93–103, 112, 116–7, 119, 145–6, 154–5
Phillips, A. 123
Piaget, J. 31–2, 94
Pleasure 144–5, 148–9, 151, 153, 155, 158
Pointon, M. 151–2
Policy-makers 57
Porter, R. 8
Post-modernism 11–2
Practice
  communities of 1, 32–3, 142, 148, 156
  Reflective 25, 73–5, 80, 83
Preferences, psychological *See 'Myers Briggs Type Indicator ®'*
Professionalism 13

Professionals, mid-career 54
Programmes, modular 91
Proximal Development, Zone of 32
Psychoanalysis *See 'Freud, Sigmund'*
Psychology, humanistic 117
Pye, E. 75, 123, 136

Quality assurance 57–8
Qualifications, Equivalent or Lower 66
Questionnaires 67–8

Referencing
  Criterion 91
  Norm 91
Reflection 50
Reflexivity 3, 24
Reification 33
Reinforcement 15
Research, ethnographic methods of 138
Retreat 38
Risk 38–9, 41, 55, 58, 59, 127
Rogers, A. 18, 24
Rogers, C. 113, 116
Rogers, J. 18
Rust, C., et al 109

Salmon, G. 48
Salzberger-Wittenberg, I., et al 118–9, 123
Scaffolding 32
Schön, D. 25, 61
Schuller, T., et al 136
Self-actualisation 112–3
Simulations 52
Skelton, A. 71
Skinner, B.F. 15
Staff and Education Development Association (SEDA) 65
Standards 55
Stress 56
System, Infra-Red Personal Response 42

Teacher
  identity of 139–40
  power of 37

professional character of 62, 78, 80, 160–1, 163
professional role of 25
professional status of 66
Teacher-centredness 8, 9, 10, 11, 12
Teaching
  awards for 71–2
  blended 53
  definition of 116
  elements of 18–26
  evaluation of 25, 50
  face-to-face 46, 48, 125–6, 135
  performance of 23–4
  preparation for 18–23
Teaching and Learning Research Programme 5
Technologies, learning 27–8, 30
Technologists, learning 27–9
Technology, Association for Learning 29
Tennant, M. 24

Theatres, lecture 42
Theory 3–4, 15
Theory and practice 3–4, 7
Thorndike, E.L. 15
Tickling 123, 126–7
Touch 123, 126
Tusting, K., and Barton, D. 16–7
Twitter 50
Type, personality *See 'Myers Briggs Type Indicator ®'*

Vygotsky, L. 31–2

Waxenegger, A. 134
Wellbeing 44, 128, 133, 136, 163
Wenger, E. 1, 32–3, 147, 148
Wiki 47
Winter, R. 74

Youell, B. 120

Zukas, M., and Malcolm, J. 70

ADULTS LEARNING
Fifth Edition

Jenny Rogers

- How do adults really learn?
- How do I handle the first class or session?
- How can I get my material across in a way that will interest and excite people?

Completely revised and updated throughout, the new edition of this friendly and practical book is the guide on how to teach adults. Written in an accessible style, it unravels the myths of teaching adults, while explaining why it is both a rewarding and a complex task.

Using case studies and examples from a wide range of sources including higher education, adult education and management development, *Adults Learning* answers questions such as:

- How do I deal with a group of mixed ability?
- How can I can I manage the conflicts that may arise in a group?
- Which teaching methods work best and which are least effective?

The author includes new chapters on problem-based learning and action learning, updated and extensive new material on handling groups, and a revised chapter on coaching, providing plenty of points for further discussion.

Adults Learning is a must-read for anyone involved in teaching adults.

Contents: *Introduction – Adult learners: what you need to know – The first session – Giving feedback – Understanding your group – Facilitating – Action learning – Problem-based learning – Coaching Role-play and simulation – Delivering information: lecturing, demonstrating and blended learning – Design for learning – Evaluating.*

2007   272pp
978-0-335-22535-4 (Paperback)

SUPPORTING LEARNERS IN THE LIFELONG LEARNING SECTOR

Marilyn Fairclough

"Marilyn Fairclough has brought her humanity, focus and gentleness to a book which will be required reading for any teacher dealing with lifelong learners. We know that many such learners are vulnerable and uncertain. The book is crammed with practical tips, is underpinned by her wisdom and wide experience and will do much to answer the question that runs through the entire book: how, exactly, do you put learners at the centre of the process at the same time as delivering a demanding curriculum?"
Jenny Rogers, Director of Management Futures Ltd, UK

"It comes as no surprise that Marilyn Fairclough has written such an excellent book. It is 'bang up to date' with her referencing of the LLUK standards. The additional references at the end of each chapter will help trainee teachers contextualise the standards and relate them to their own teaching practice."
Paula Kavanagh, Aylesbury College, UK

"Having recently taught the new PTLLS and CTLLS qualifications I wish that this book had been available to recommend to learners working towards achieving these qualifications."
Ian Grant, Milton Keynes Adult Continuing Education, UK

Welcome to *Supporting Learners in the Lifelong Learning Sector* – the first book of its kind to deal with the topic of *supporting* learners in PCET, rather than just focussing on how to teach them.

This friendly and accessible book stresses the significance of support at each stage of the learning process to minimize learner drop-out and underachievement. It considers a broad range of support that learners may need from their tutors, from making a choice of learning programme to their exit and progression to further learning or employment.

Key features include:

- 'Something to Think About' at the beginning of every chapter
- Each chapter cross-referenced to the QTLS Professional Standard for those on PTLLS, CTLLS and DTLLS courses
- Real life examples from a variety of settings and subjects
- Lots of useful tips and ideas to ensure that all learners receive appropriate support
- Practical suggestions for developing classroom practice
- Suggestions for managing disruptive behaviour
- Thought-provoking activities and reflection points

Contents: *Preface – Acknowledgements – Abbreviations – Introduction – Who are the learners? – Who gives support? – What's the point of theory? – What do we need to know about learners? – Getting the relationships right – Planning for individual needs – How much do they remember? – Assessment – Evaluating learning – involving the learners – Communicating: what message are they getting? – Personal problems – Behavioural problems – Disability barriers – Cultural awareness – Appendices – Bibliography – Index.*

2008   176pp
978-0-335-23362-5 (Paperback)   978-0-335-23363-2 (Hardback)

A TOOLKIT FOR CREATIVE TEACHING IN POST-COMPULSORY EDUCATION

Linda Eastwood, Jennie Coates, Liz Dixon, Josie Harvey, Chris Ormondroyd and Sarah Williamson

- Are you looking for ways to encourage learners to think more creatively?
- Do you need ideas for fun and engaging activities for individuals and groups?
- Would you like a practical step-by-step guide written by practitioners *for* practitioners?

YES? Then this is the book for you!

This is the essential resource for trainees and teachers working in the PCET sector who are looking for new and creative ways of engaging and motivating their learners.

The book contains 50 brilliant activities that can be used in a variety of settings and applied to different subject areas. The authors give specific details relating to planning, preparation and implementation for each activity and, in addition, suggest a whole range of further variations for each activity to try out too!

Key features include:

- 50 practical and innovative teaching activities
- Practical tips to get the most from each activity
- Variations and subject-specific examples
- Thinking Points to encourage reflection
- What Next signposts to further reading
- A theoretical framework which sets the activities within the context of creativity and innovation

A Toolkit for Creative Teaching in Post-Compulsory Education is an essential handbook for teacher training students and for new and experienced teachers undertaking Professional Development.

Contents: *List of Contributors – Acknowledgements – Introduction – Part I Practical Activities – Text-Free Teaching – Radio Interviews – Who Do You Think You Are? – Dominoes – In the Bag – Using Models and Metaphors – The Learning Cafe – On the One Hand – Learning Laundry Line – Terminology Bingo – A Card to Remember – Menu Cards – Learning Party – Board Games – Odd Opposites – Get Physical – Learning Carousel – Using Recipes – Censored! – Censored! – I'm in Charge – Speed Networking – Organizing an Event – Rainbow Groups – Just a Minute – Film Festival – Explain to the Aliens – E-Treasure Hunt – Jigsaws – Problem Page – Using Puppets – Learning Landscapes – Memory Box – Learning Dice – Learning Ladders – Roving Reporters – In the Frame – In the Mood for Music – Web Chat: Online Discussion Groups – Changing Rooms – Character Biography Cards – Wear Your Learning – Headaches and Aspirins – Wikis at Work – Paper Chains – Cluster Cards – Market Square – Learning Mats – Learning Museums – Ask the Expert – Inside Outside – Part II Theoretical Framework – Creativity – Bibliography – Index.*

2009   144pp
978-0-335-23416-5 (Paperback)   978-0-335-23415-8 (Hardback)